The Soul of a Single Parent

How to Snapback and Get Your SWAG On

APRIL BOYD-NORONHA

Single Parent Life Strategist

authorHOUSE®

AuthorHouse™ LLC
1663 Liberty Drive
Bloomington, IN 47403
www.authorhouse.com
Phone: 1-800-839-8640

Published by AuthorHouse   03/26/2014

ISBN: 978-1-4918-9838-3 (sc)
ISBN: 978-1-4918-9837-6 (e)

Library of Congress Control Number: 2014905548

Contents

Acknowledgement Page

This book is dedicated to:

My three children—Zaria, Nyah and Caleb.

My mother, Clarissa, who taught me all there is to know about successful single parenting.

The "real" single parents who truly understand their divine role of raising their children.

I am grateful to God for everything.

Introduction

I know you're asking yourself, how can I snapback as a single parent? I'm not even sure if I got any SWAG left, let alone a Single Parent SWAG? I know, I know. You're looking at your situation saying to yourself—I'm living paycheck to paycheck. Some days you don't know whether you're coming or going. Most days you're a minute away from a meltdown. Nowadays, you feel so alone and life is <u>never</u> fair. Yesterday, you just didn't care. Today isn't much better. It seems like you're just going through the motions. You're sick and tired of sacrificing for everybody else—but YOU! "Stressed" has become your new middle name. "Emotional" is your 2nd new middle name. Nothing makes sense or adds up (especially when it comes to your money). You've got mouths to feed, bodies to clothe, and no time to take care of **YOU**! You stretch yourself so thin, you can barely recognize yourself in the mirror. You're tired of waiting on your "whenever, whatever" because of so many empty promises. You try not to get caught up in the mess, but the mess seems to follow you home. SWAG? What SWAG? More like single parent hag (let's keep it real)! Your SWAG left the building so many years ago when your self-esteem hit the floor. Your SWAG went M-I-A when D-A-D went B-Y-E.

But hold up, wait a minute, slow your roll! From one single parent to another, I'm here to tell you that it **is** possible to get your SWAG back. I've been there, done that, bought the ticket, lost the ticket, then found the ticket wedged way down in between the seats in my minivan. Since you are a single parent, you are *required* to snapback and get your SWAG back. Didn't you know that's one of the top five rules in the Single Parent Handbook (ok, not really, but you get the picture)?! Seriously, successful single parenting depends on one critical person—you, the single parent.

Honestly, I admit at times I hate it when I am "the one". You know, the:

. . . Single parent with one or more kids "in tow" at all times (I have three kids)

. . . Mom in the group with no ring on her finger or no mate sitting nearby

. . . Parent who's late to most events because you're juggling schedules and/or special events for all of your children

. . . Parent who's the last to pick up your child because you're fighting fatigue or got off work late

. . . Mom who's not quite as "pulled together" or polished as the other moms because that's an expense that requires a 2nd income

. . . Parent that's always the "sole cheerleader" at all of your child's events

. . . Recipient of the patronizing conversation and stares because you have nothing in common with "them" (the married ones)

. . . "habitual dater" with many suitors vs. date nights with your spouse

. . . Parent that experiences the looks of pity when you enter the room

. . . Parent that puts up with the looks of disbelief from other parents when you pull up in the parking lot in your hooptie

But there is hope! Yes, even against these odds, you still can snap back and get your S.W.A.G. on! And the time is NOW!!

"The Soul of a Single Parent" is a candid, up-close-and-personal perspective of my journey as a single parent. I purposely did not include a chapter listing the latest facts and statistics regarding single parenting. Honestly, much of this so-called documented data is depressing, demeaning and quite frankly do not represent many of today's single parent homes. I know much of the latest reports does not reflect <u>my</u> single parent principles and the environment at which I raise my three children.

"The Soul of a Single Parent" is written from a single *mom's* perspective. This is not to discount, disregard or discredit the many single fathers who also single-handedly choose to "do the right thing" every day. I personally know a few of them and I fully support and applaud their efforts. Within the universal single parent dialogue, single fathers are the unsung heroes and do not get the credit due. Their single parenting efforts are regularly overlooked, rarely regarded, if even ever acknowledged. So, I want to take a moment to salute the fathers who choose to single parent sons and especially their daughters each and every day.

Now, there are many definitions floating out there of what a single parent is today. So, let me take a moment to explain *my* definition of a single parent. A single parent: 1) is not living with a spouse or partner as the result of separation, death, child abuse/neglect, or divorce, 2) is primarily dependent on their/one <u>consistent</u> form of income, 3) may receive child support and/or alimony, 4) may qualify for government assistance because you fall within the "poverty" income level, 5) is the sole or primary caregiver of one or more dependent children, and 6) has been granted full custody and has all rights in making all decisions regarding your children, ex. medical, school, residence, etc.

A *"true"* single parent is <u>NOT</u>: a spouse whose mate is deployed or temporarily relocated. The difference here is that there still is <u>unconditional</u> support available between the two parents—financial, emotional, decision making, responsibilities, real expectations in regards to their role (mother/father), etc. For those who choose to disagree with my definition, let me put it this way. When I was a military spouse or when my former husband was a government contractor, even when he was away I knew funds would always be available to take care of any needed family expenses. I still had access to *disposable* income to take the kids out to dinner every Friday. Or even in his absence, I still had the *luxury* to splurge on weekend activities with the kids "just because". Single parents tend *not* to have much disposable income. Nor do they *frequently* have the luxury to splurge "just because". **This** is the difference between "real" single parenting and simply *feeling* like you are a single parent for only a few days, weeks, or months out of the year.

The following chapters are but a glimpse of the journey into the soul of a single parent. Unless you are truly a single parent, don't judge me until you have walked *at least* a mile in my shoes or spent a _whole_ day—no scratch that—a whole week, in the life of a single parent. If you are a single parent, I hope you enjoy this literary journey with me. Feel free to laugh (_with_ me, not _at_ me) as you read through the pages. Go ahead, sit down and shed a tear of joy (or pain) with me as I share my world with you. More importantly, I pray that you gain further insight and purpose as to your divine role as a single parent. Each chapter will start with my perspective or a short snippet of "coming from where I'm from". Then I will dig deeper and further share "my truth or turning point" of my single parent journey. Are you ready to snapback from single parent paralysis? Is it time to get your SWAG on? If so, then let's begin!

Single Parent Access

Coming From Where I'm From:

Because you are a single parent, access to information will be kept from you—intentionally. You WILL be counted out, once you disclose your marital status—SINGLE parent. No, it's not your imagination that this "less than, why even bother" mindset exists. Even worse it will trickle down to your children as well. So be prepared for teachers, administrators, school systems, and *even* counselors to have low expectations of you and your level of involvement in regards to your child's education—from Day One. Sad to say, the stigma prevails in today's educational system that a child is automatically doomed to fail if they're raised in a single parent home. Well, I'm here to tell you, as a single parent, I prove them wrong **every day**.

My Truth/Turning Point:

I vividly remember an elementary school teacher I had. Now in hindsight, as an adult, I realize that she literally persecuted me every day that I set foot into her classroom. It was made very clear (non-verbally) that she did not want me in her classroom. In her attempts to torment me, it seemed like on a daily basis she pitted me against male, well-dressed, privileged students while answering math problems on the chalkboard in the front of the room. As if her intimidation and bullying wasn't enough, when I would time after time again defeat her diabolical attacks, she would ignore me for the rest of the day. Now, here's where strategic single parenting is crucial. When I confessed the injustices to my mother, she didn't race to the school and demand a conference with that teacher. Instead, she sat with me and explained "the big picture". Since she was an educator herself, she was fully aware of the power of a teacher and possible racism that I might face at such a tender age. But she also reminded me that in the long run, this boot camp experience will have been well worth it. Next, we devised a strategy: 1) have open, ongoing and consistent communication about my day with my mother— the debriefing/interrogation phase and 2) adjust my attitude, plan, tactics, etc. as needed—the implementation phase. Yes, my MOS (the US Army term for Military Occupational Specialty) became Special Forces! Just kidding, but you get the point. The harsh reality was I knew my mother could not be there protecting me 24/7. She was a single parent who had to work in order to provide for me. But what she DID do was encourage me during every minute of the drive until we arrived at the steps of the school. Each day we were like soldiers planning tactical strategy (get a quality education) to defeat the enemy (teachers, the system). Through it all, she made sure that I never felt defeated, yet was ready to defend my right to be a student to learn just as any of the other students. My mission was clear: 1) go to school, 2) get a **quality** education, and 3) apply the knowledge and experiences (the sometimes good, mostly bad, and very ugly) I learned *as a child* to successfully deal with real world obstacles, *as an adult*. Yes, Momma, it was well worth it.

Now, I will break from protocol and admit, there have been rare occasions, where "the others" (teachers, moms who were married, the system) were truly committed to the cause and "showed me the way." It was on the low-low, but nevertheless, they reached out and I gratefully received the message. Now, as a single parent, I had a choice to make. Remember the 95% of the times "the others" they made me feel like the scum of the earth. OR "suck it up" and look at the big picture—by any means necessary, ensure the successful transition of my child at school using the intel provided 5% of the time.

But maybe you have very limited access to information—you work long hours, varying work schedules, health issues, language/culture barriers, little or no support from family/friends, etc. Just like anything else, where there's a will, there's a way! Go online and see what resources are available on the school district website and/or the teacher's site. Yes, it takes more time that you *already* don't have. I get that, really I do. But remember, as single parents, sacrifice *now* in order to have success *later* (ex. a child that graduates – on time, is accepted into college, has employable work skills, etc.). Single parents have got to think LONG TERM. It's not about this semester or year, it's about getting them to their final year. It's not about "wishful thinking" that they're doing okay at school, it's about you checking his/her folder each night (or every other day or weekly) to see their work and quickly respond to teacher requests/notes. It's not about hoping they get the "right" teacher, it's about arranging to have them taught by a teacher that connects with **you** as a single parent, too. Even if that means requesting to have your child transferred to another classroom. I know, let me pause for a minute. As a single parent, you must keep your eyes on the prize—a successful school year for your child. So, forget the emotions. Put your feelings aside. And handle your business. It is about **your** child getting access to the "best" teacher and school system that is equipped to deal with single parent household concerns.

Not only is it important for you to focus on your child's ongoing education, but what about yours? As a single parent, there are job training facilities that provide access to free training. If you don't have time to sit in a classroom, there are many online resources to learn something new that can help to increase your financial situation. Attending a class for 18 months or 2 years is nothing compared to a substantial increase in pay over a lifetime. THINK LONG TERM!

Single parent access *today*, has long-term effects for *tomorrow*!

Single Parent Affirmation

It is SO important that you affirm your single parent journey by using positive sayings, inspirational songs that celebrate your single parent snapback or any other form of communication that uplifts your soul—a favorite movie, book, special moments in life, etc. Listed below are a few of mine. Highlight or put a checkmark next to those that are *your* favorites, too! Or add some of your own.

SONGS:

1) "The Battle is the Lord's" by Yolanda Adams (Live in Washington cd)
2) "Keep On Moving" by Soul II Soul
3) "Single Life" by Cameo
4) "Living My Life Like It's Golden" by Jill Scott
5) "Miss Independent" by Ne-Yo
6) "Single" by Ne-Yo
7) "Champagne Life" by Ne-Yo
8) "She's Got Her Own" by Ne-Yo
9) "New Attitude" by Patti LaBelle
10) "I Wanna Be Free" by Patti LaBelle (Tyler Perry's "Diary of a Mad Black Woman" movie soundtrack)
11) "Struggle No More" by Anthony Hamilton (Tyler Perry's Daddy's Little Girls" movie soundtrack)

12) "I Can Do Bad All By Myself" by Mary J Blige (Tyler Perry's "I Can Do Bad All By Myself" movie soundtrack)
13) "Not Gon Cry" by Mary J Blige ("Waiting To Exhale" movie soundtrack)
14) "It's Not Right, But It's Okay" by Whitney Houston
15) "Pearls" by Sade
16) "Skin" by Sade
17) "Soldier of Love" by Sade
18) "I Got Work To Do" by Vanessa Williams
19) "Hate on Me" by Jill Scott
20) "Wanna Be Loved" by Jill Scott
21) "Slo Woman" by Mint Condition
22) Erykah Badu: Live cd. Any song by her.
23) List your favorite _____
24) List your favorite _____

MOVIES:

1) That moment in "The Matrix" when Neo realizes he is "the one".
2) The scene in "The Baby Boom" when JC realizes she's got to do it (single parenting) on her own if she is gonna make it.
3) The moment in "Hope Floats" when Birdie realizes that Justin really does like/love her—just for being her.
4) The frustration chronicled by the four women in the movie "Set It Off".
5) The journey of renewal and love experienced by Joanna after betrayal by her husband in the movie "Sex & Mrs. X".
6) The moment in the movie "Gloria" (1980, featuring Gena Rowlands) when she realizes that she has to assume the mother figure for six-year old Phil.
7) List your favorite _____
8) List your favorite _____

QUOTES:

1) "Time waits for no man (or woman)."
2) "Today is the first day of the rest of your life."
3) List your favorite _____
4) List your favorite _____

PEOPLE:

Public figures who were raised in a single parent home, is a single parent or who are/were consistent champions for children raised in single parent households.

1) Marion Wright Edelman—Die hard defender and children's activist, founder of the Children's Defense Fund.
2) Nelson Mandela—Human rights activist who always considered the future (children, legacy) when determining his current actions/decisions.
3) President Barack Obama—Went from being raised in a single parent home to leading America's homes every day.
4) Harriet Tubman—Abolitionist, humanitarian. Instrumental in freeing of slaves, knowing that freedom was the key to keeping a family together.
5) Recording artist Sade—A single mom, no further explanation needed, really!
6) Actress/former Miss America Vanessa Williams—A single mom, the epitome of the "snapback/comeback queen"!
7) Natalie Hawkins—Mother of Gabrielle Douglas, 2-time US Women's Gymnastics Gold Medalist.
8) List your favorite _____
9) List your favorite _____

BOOKS:

1) "Too Blessed to Be Stressed" by Dr. Suzan D. Johnson Cook
2) "Guide My Feet" by Marion Wright Edelman

3) "Hard Questions, Heart Answers" by The Reverend Bernice A. King
4) "The Prayer of Jabez" by Bruce Wilkinson
5) "The Measure of Our Success" by Marion Wright Edelman
6) "Give It Back!" by Kimberly Daniels
7) "Woman Thou Art Loosed" by TD Jakes
8) List your favorite _____
9) List your favorite _____

Look into your soul and affirm your single parent lifestyle!

Single Parent Bitterness

Coming From Where I'm From: One night while wallowing in my abyss of bitterness, I called a mentor of mine. Normally I wouldn't have called her to talk about my personal business (she was my business coach), but I remembered that at one time she had been a single parent, too. Her life, now, looked pretty darn nice—she's married, in a thriving career that she loves, living in a custom built home, travels the world, etc. I pleaded with her to help me keep holding on! I needed a word of encouragement from a single parent who had "been there and done that." She testified that she once was caught up in a turbulent, abusive relationship with her daughter's father. It was at that very moment that my own transformation from bitter to better began as she revealed simple, yet strategic steps she took for her transformation from stuck to successful. You never know where someone's been. But there is a journey we are all trying to *endure* and ultimately *enjoy* along the way. One thing for sure, each journey is unique.

My Truth/Turning Point: One turning point during this conversation stood out in my mind. She encouraged me every day to pray for, forgive, and <u>consciously</u> think about the positive things that took place in the relationship with my ex-husband. Now, at first I thought this lady is crazy! At that point in my life I was swimming in misery, loneliness, and disbelief. Didn't she just hear me pour out my heart explaining all that this fool just put me through?! But through all my pouting, denial, and whining she continued to remind me that nothing was going to get better until I changed FROM my bitterness mentality TO a better thought process filled with forgiveness. By now, I was at the point of hanging up on her (but I couldn't because I still needed her to coach me on business ideas). So, I ended our conversation by being silent, using my classic passive-aggressive behavior. After a few days of walking around in defiance, I decided to give her advice a try. I took out a notebook and began to journal. Each day, I made a conscious effort to write about, meditate on, and send positive mental energy to all the hurt, betrayal, lies, and mess that had entered into my life over the last 10 years during my marriage, separation and divorce. Some days I could only muster up a few words to write. Other days I poured my heart out. This transformation from bitter to better was a serious daily battle for me. My flesh wanted to hate my ex, but I knew I had a choice to make— be **better** or be **bitter**. Let me repeat that—I HAD A CHOICE TO MAKE! Plus, when I looked at the life of my mentor, she was living the life I wanted to live one day, someday! So, I knew it was possible. And if it's possible for her, it's possible for **me**. If it's possible for me, then it's definitely possible for **you**, too! Choose wisely.

*Wanna learn more about my journey from bitter to better? Contact me via email at **april@singleparentliving.net** to get started on your journey.*

Look into your soul and release the bitterness!

Single Parent Choices/Decisions

Coming From Where I'm From: The moment I realized I was REALLY a single parent was when I had to stretch ONE income to feed and care for FOUR people. I decided that every decision had to be "the one"—the one that mattered most. Gone were the days of disposable income, or depending on a sizeable second income. Now *every* darn penny spent had to count. As a single parent, even the people that you let deposit their time, plans/ideas, and money into you and your household, matters. If the return on investment is worth it, then keep them in your life. But if they are making more withdraws than deposits—let them go and keep walking. And if they don't want to go, then you get up and run the other way. Notice I didn't say walk—I said *run*. Yes, sometimes you gotta run, with what you have at that very moment, because you know it's about to go down. But as a single parent, you cannot afford to let a bad situation get worse or more violent than it already is. Even when we don't think our kids are watching or listening—they are! We may think they're not affected by their environment, but they are.

My Truth/Turning Point: Choose you this day—life or death. If you're reading this book, you have chosen to LIVE! I remember, like it was yesterday, the day I decided to leave my ex. I was crushed, felt defeated, depleted, at my wits end—all at the same time. With each box I packed, I cried a river of tears—of sorrow and of joy. But the lesson in that moment was this: now, from this day forth, I must determine to what extent I am going to let someone/something positively or negatively impact my life—and ultimately my children's lives. I accessed my situation and did what I had to do—pack our things and leave. And I haven't looked back, not once. Each day you must be proactive in your position on matters—personally, professionally, spiritually, mentally, financially, etc. Get into the mindset of asking yourself "Is this working FOR me or AGAINST me? Will a decision help me get to my goal or move me further away from it? Does this mate or friend help or hurt me when I need them the most? How do these actions/reactions impact my life—positively or negatively? As the saying goes, if "Today is the first day of the rest of your life", then what are you going to do to make it the BEST day of the rest of your life? As a single parent, you must think beyond today. As a matter of fact, you must think 10 to 20 years down the line. With every waking moment, you are faced with the daunting task of asking "Where do I see myself in the future?" Equally, if not more importantly, is the question "Where do I see my *child(ren)* in 10 to 20 years from now? You are the key to getting them "there"— wherever their "there" may be. No guts, no glory. Now is the time to "suck it up" and show up (be there) in your child's life. The parental groundwork must be laid in the early years of your child's life in order to see the "proof in the pudding" in later years. With every decision made while single parenting, you must weigh the pros vs. the cons. Then and only then can you gain clarity and serenity in your journey towards successful single parenting.

Look into your soul and choose wisely!

Single Parent Commitment

Coming From Where I'm From: Being raised in a single parent home by my mother, one thing I knew for sure was that she was committed to raising me. In comparison, as a single parent of three kids, I know it was "easier" for her. But the point is she was always there. When I went to bed—she was there. When I woke up in the morning—she was there. When I had a sports or school event—she was there. When I asked—she was there. Now, no, my mom was not superwoman (even though to this day I say she is). But for those times when she was dog tired, she had my grandparents as her "back up, to the back up" plan. So, considering all things, I was "lucky" to have been raised as a single child. Now as a single parent, of THREE children, I understand the real value of *being there*. But I fight the temptation to give up as I sacrifice and struggle with the daily juggling of the schedules of four people.

My Truth/Turning Point: So, what is a single parent to do? During one of our family meetings, I promised my kids that I was committed to the following four things:

1) Making sure they were grounded in Christian principles. I know I would not be here without the same principles that my mother instilled in me, come hell or high water every Sunday, Wednesday, Thursday and Saturday. I see you nodding and agreeing as you have your own flashbacks of the good ole' church days.

2) Helping them excel in school in every subject and extracurricular activity that they truly want to pursue. If it means getting a tutor or staying up late to do/check their homework—then that's what it was. If it means making 2 to 3 trips to their school or late nights for after school events, then that's what it means. If it means sacrificing "me time" extras in order to pay for an instrument or lessons, then that's what it is.

3) Providing their <u>basic</u> needs (not wants)—food, clothes and shelter for survival. Now let me explain. This doesn't mean buying name brand clothes at full price at the mall every weekend. No, we strategically shop consignment and thrift shops and accept donated clothes from friends (who can afford name brand clothes for *their* children) who have now outgrown them. I have no problem with being a recipient of the "Pay It Forward" principle. There is no shame in the game of a "real" single parent. I'm just saying.

4) Making sure they knew—without a shadow of a doubt—that they were my priority, at all times. Ok, well at least 99% of the time. Can I *at least* get 1% to myself, please? My children don't need yet another parent to make them feel as if they were not worthy of being #1. With every decision that I make, I remind my children that *that* decision is for a) *their* good—individually; b) *our* good—as a family; and c) *MY* good as their mother and sole provider who is counting down the days until they leave the house and become self-sufficient! But I digress, let's stay focused here, right?! My children understand that just as they expect me to be committed to their needs, I expect them to be equally, if not more loyal to living up to their part of being committed to me as their parent and sole provider. If I'm providing a spiritually nurturing environment of respect and honor, then the level of R-E-S-P-E-C-T and honor in our home better be at its highest at all times. I better feel like the Queen of Honor in my house. When things are not going so well, they better bust out in a prayer instead of a temper tantrum or foul-mouth explosion of emotions in order to shift the situation. If I promise to help them excel in school, they better bring home A's and B's or perform

at their top level of sports or music events. Since I "bring home the bacon AND fry it up in a pan" they better appreciate a home cooked meal or as they get older and prove themselves responsible, with prior approval, cook the darn meal and have it ready for *me* when I get home! OK?! Since I buy the clothes, they can keep them off the floor and when old enough wash the clothes, too. I promise to have laundry detergent, broom and a vacuum if they promise to keep their rooms clean. Seriously, this level of commitment is a learned skill. Your kids might as well learn it at home with people who really care about them. That way, they won't be too heartbroken or surprised when they realize they can't depend on others in the "real world" when outside of the safe haven of home.

Look into your soul and commit to your single parent life!

Single Parent Confidence

Coming From Where I'm From: EVERY single parent needs an *extra* daily dose of confidence to combat all the haters out there conspiring to keep single parents "down and out". Either we are bombarded daily by receiving the negative news from the latest reports and statistics on single parenting or we get "sucka-punched" by the stigma of living a single parent lifestyle while trying to get ahead. But "ooh ooh child", things have got to get better and brighter. But it depends on YOU!

My Truth/Turning Point: I know you're thinking "I can't worry about one more thing. I'm already at my point of popping it off up in here!" As a single parent, I'll give you that. I've been there and done that—and after all was said and done, it came down to me looking at myself in the mirror. And as I did, you know what I noticed? I noticed little ole' ME! I noticed the skin tone of my face—pimples, blemishes and all that. I looked into those tired eyes, though they looked sad, they still had a little spark in them. I looked at my breast, they were small, but still perky, baby! I looked at my belly, a little bulge there, but I can live with that, for real! I saw my battle scars of bringing life into this world three times—stretch marks have a story to tell. I looked down at my legs—long and lean (from chasing after my kids or trying to keep up with our family's weekly schedule of events). By the time I got to my feet, I marveled at how my frame effortlessly settled at the base of my size 8 1/2 AAA narrow feet. It was at that moment that I said to myself "If this is all I got to work with, then let's work it, baby!" Yes, I really said that to myself.

DISCLAIMER: It's ok to talk to yourself, as long as you don't hear yourself talking back. I stepped back from the mirror to get one last, long look at ME. I took it all in. The small butt, long legs, big forehead, slightly bucked teeth from being a thumb sucker until 3rd grade—all of ME. It was as if I was looking at a new ME. And you know what? I was. I was looking at the new, single parent ME. And she didn't look as bad as I thought! I gave myself a "hi-five" and skipped away from the mirror. Yes, I actually did a hop:skip combo as I exited the room. Yet, here's the deal. I am what I am. It is what it is. But I know that I know that I can be better. It sure can be a lot worse. So, I'm gonna work with what I got to work with—and celebrate ME every day! I'm gonna appreciate ME, even if no one else will. I am ready to love—love me, that is!

Need help in taking that first step of single parent confidence? Contact me for coaching or mentoring at april@singleparentliving.net.

It's time to snapback and get your SWAG on!

Single Parent Dating

Coming From Where I'm From: When I first ventured back into dating, my mind was not *really* ready. But my body was (ya'll know what I mean)! So, even though I was open to the world of dating again I was still very guarded and extremely untrusting of men. On a scale of 1 to 10 (where 10 is a "Hell No!"), I was at a 9.3! Couple that with being extremely lonely and too impatient for the moons to align up just right so I could find Mr. Right—I found myself bouncing from "friend-to-friend" and empty relationships that were more physical than meaningful.

My Truth/Turning Point: So, essentially I was "playing the field" because I sure wasn't about to get played again. Yep, I had it down to a fine science. It went a little something like this:

Step #1: Each potential mate had to go through my pro vs. con list. The Pro's (or positives) consisted of: have a job, own/rent their own home, be healthy, have a sexy physique, be responsible (pay his own bills) i.e., takes care of his Momma/sister, handy around the house. The Con's (or negatives) consisted of: have no kids younger than the ages of mine, NO baby momma drama. It's only fair since I had no baby daddy drama. I know that seems like a lot, but hey, I might as well be strategic about this and put my MBA to work, right?

Step #2: Group my dating prospects into three categories:

A) "Old Friend"—this is the safest category because I have a solid history with these guys. I either grew up with them in the neighborhood or our families know each other. When we hook up, we can reminisce about the good ole days while making new memories.

B) "The Want Me's"—these are the guys who I knew wanted *me* more than I wanted *them*. They may also fall into the "Old Friend" category or may be someone I met online. The point here is to maintain control. So, most of the time they were long-distance relationships, online friendships or some other *detached* form of friendship, and

C) "Casual Acquaintance"—this type of dating is self-explanatory; where you and the potential mate determine, up front, what the conditions of your meeting/friendship were going to be. When you're in public—you are "just friends". When at functions and you bump in to each other—you are "just friends". If ever you are together in a room with your kids—you are "just friends". When you are alone—you are "just friends", but with benefits. Kind of like the characters Marcus (Eddie Murphy) and Jacqueline (Robin Givens) in the movie Boomerang. The key is to keep it simple. If it gets complicated, all bets are off—unless you BOTH agree otherwise. You must always be willing to turn around and walk away, with no regrets and definitely no drama. This type of dating is only for the grown and sexy. Ladies, it has been known to bring out the "stalker" in some men. I have enough experiences that I could write my 3rd book on surviving stalkers. So, when I say "Play at your own risk!", I mean it, seriously!

Now, I know this seems exciting, all fun and games—and it was, for a minute! But that's all it is—fun and games. But real life has to kick in some time, right? One day I woke up after all the stalker phone calls and emails and thought "Is this all there is?" I decided to take myself out of the game and focus on me, myself, and I. The reality was I wasn't just single. I was a single <u>parent</u>, too, with three kids to raise and too much at stake.

Interested in learning how I went from loosely dating to loving myself?
*Contact me to discuss your coaching plan at **april@singleparentliving.net**.*

Single parent dating is fine as long as you have some "do's and don'ts" in place!

Single Parent Destiny

Coming From Where I'm From: Your destiny is determined by you. Sure there are distractions, detours, pitfalls and potholes along the way. Some of these all happen in just one day—the inevitable "day from hell". Most days like this are deliberate—plots from coworkers, haters, etc. Other situations come out of nowhere—as fate would have it. Some are subconsciously brought about by you (ex. fear of success, procrastination). Other circumstances can be avoided, yet you deliberately "fall on the sword" in your moment of "single parent martyrdom". But putting all the drama aside, for the most part, <u>you</u> still hold the key to your success or failure. It all depends on how bad you want it—for yourself and your children.

My Truth/Turning Point: As a single child, raised in a single parent home, I learned early on to see things as black and white. To this day, I cannot function well within gray areas. I live by this principle and hold others, especially my family and close friends, to this high level of expectations, as well. One way I gain clarity in this process is by using reasoning tools such as "If-Then" statements, pros vs. cons lists, t-charts, forecasting to determine the possible consequences, anticipating the distractions, and planning for moments of procrastination, to name a few. Even though there is no crystal ball to peer into the future, instead of being *reactive* and just letting whatever happen, happen; choose to be proactive and possibly prevent the *seemingly* inevitable. As single parents, you cannot afford to *only* have a Plan A and a Plan B. Oh no! You must always have a Plan C, D, E, F, and G—just in case. I'm just keeping it real.

*Are you ready to take that first step towards your single parent destiny? Contact me at **april@singleparentliving.net**.*

Only *YOU* can determine your destiny!

Single Parent Dreams . . . Deferred

Coming From Where I'm From: Wake up and wait no more for that magical mate to mysteriously make it all right! Do it now & do it well . . . by yourself, in the meantime. A dream deferred is the most dangerous stage of life to exist. Living in limbo leaves you at odds with yourself—you're neither coming nor going; simply running around in circles. The key is to remember that a "not *now*" status doesn't necessarily mean a "not *ever*" situation. Anything is possible. You've got to believe enough for it to come to pass (whatever your "it" is). Stop *speaking* against it (your dreams, goals, aspiration) and stop *thinking* defeating thoughts about your future. Consciously ask yourself "Do I hear the words coming out of my mouth?" On a daily basis, recognize, reflect, and respond to what you are speaking *over* and *in* your life. Never underestimate the amount of power YOU have in bringing your dreams to reality—sooner than you think. But as you are reflecting, be careful not to let people mistake your silence for being a "sucka". All that matters is that **you** know you're fully aware of what's going on. So, take a moment to process the situation; others may see you as passive or a punk. But "Au contraire, mon frère" (French phrase that means "on the contrary, my brother"). It really doesn't matter what they think anyway. It's *your* dream. It's *your* life. It's time to stop dreaming and LIVE!!

The Truth/Turning Point: Are you constantly driving by your dream house? Go ahead and buy or even build it—if you can afford it. If you don't have the funds to do it now, discover ways to make your dream come true—drive on by the drive thru or catch a movie at home instead. It's the little things that add up and keep you moving further away from your dreams. Do you slow down when you pass the car lot that displays your dream car? Make that dream a reality and buy that car—if it is in your price range! Once again, there are strategic steps that you can begin to take *today* in order to have that car *tomorrow*. Are your eyes glued to the TV every time that commercial comes on about your favorite vacation spot? Go for it. Book that vacation spot you've been dying to see—if your finances can fit it in. The old adage still applies "Time waits for no man—or woman."

Don't let a *"single parent"* income hold you back. Yes, it may take you a little longer than others to save up since there's only one income, but it will be worth it. Many single parents are successful at making a dollar out of 50 cents; miraculously stretching the amount of money they have as the sole provider of their household. It's all about a good mix of timing, saving and planning!

Do you have a story to tell? Write about it as an author, blogger, or columnist. Who knows? Your book could be the answer to another single parent's dilemma. Your blog could be the link to someone's life being turned around. Your column could be featured at just the right time with just the right message to turn a reader's life around.

Are you a walking testimony? Tell someone about it. Let others be a witness to your success story. Empower other single parents by letting them know they are not alone. Inspire others by showing them that if you did "it" (whatever your "it" is) then they can do it too! If you survived amidst devastating everyday struggles and are still alive to tell your story, then you are destined to "do the right thing" and tell it. You can share your testimony while speaking from a podium or sitting next to someone on a pew. Your mission is to share your story to positively encourage others.

Whatever your goal(s); whichever format you choose to share your story, the key is to **do it now and do it well**. Timing is of essence. Procrastination is the "thorn in the side" of every single parent. Seize the moment! Brush your shoulders off! Shake the dust off your feet! Wipe the crust from your eyes! Now go handle your business!

*Need help in taking that first step? Don't know where to go from here? Contact me for coaching or mentoring at **april@singleparentliving.net**.*

Look into your soul and dream BIG!

Single Parent Faith

Coming From Where I'm From: When it comes to faith, I'm reminded of the lyrics of a song that was sung many times while growing up in my Baptist church. The lyrics are: "If it had not been for the Lord, where would I be? Where would I be?" As a child, I didn't fully understand the truth in these words. But now as a single parent, there have been many times when I rocked myself to sleep in the comfort of my own arms, while humming these words softly to put my soul at rest. Your life must be God-centered because you <u>cannot</u> do it alone. There will be times where you will need supernatural, spiritual guidance against predators, manipulators, vultures, opportunists—in your family, within your home, at your workplace, in society, online, next door. ANYONE, ANYWHERE.

My Truth/Turning Point: My truth about the principle of faith is that it is the firm belief in what you can't see or touch, yet knowing, without a shadow of a doubt, that all is *still* possible. But in order to see the impossible *become* possible, you must commit to the following:

1) Have a "no **F**ear" mindset.
2) **A**llow God to do His part.
3) **I**dentify the promises of God.
4) **T**rust in His perfect Will and His divine Way.
5) **H**ope beyond what your current situation may be at this particular moment.

Yes, faith requires a lot of action. As a single parent, you must be prepared to take action, even when it *seems* as if you are taking 10 steps backward. Alignment with the Will of God is a crucial factor in testing one's faith. Knowing *what* to ask for, *when* to ask for it and being open to freely receive it, can and should be as simple as when your own children asks something of you. Will you deny them what they want, especially if they have been obedient and patient? No! God is the same way and even more lenient towards you because you are His child. Since He is sovereign, just think how much *more* He wants to give you. But you can only receive according to your level of faith and dependence on Him. Are you ready to receive all the blessings He has stored up for you? Stop trying to do it your way (the hard way) and cast your cares; in other words, let God handle it. Your blessings are there for the receiving, but only if you have faith enough to believe and be open to receive. Do you believe? Are you truly ready to receive?

Single parent F.A.I.T.H. is the <u>foundation</u> for single parent living!

Single Parent Fantasy

Coming From Where I'm From: Sometimes there's a fine line between fantasy and reality; especially when you want something or someone SO bad. Blurred lines get in the way and you can't tell right from wrong because it feels so good to be bad. Single parents cannot afford the luxury of living in a world of fantasy. The real world ain't no joke. It'll remind you that times are hard when the bills are due *today* but payday isn't until *next* week. Real life will bum rush you so hard it'll have you going in circles trying to make a dollar out of 50 cents until the end of the month. Have you been at the point that you were hanging on the ledge *not* by your finger*tips*, but by your very finger*nails;* and they were bitten down so bad from stressing out, that you barely had any nails left?

My Truth/Turning Point: I love the twist on single parenting that the movie "Baby Boom" explores. It stars Diane Keaton (one of my favorite actresses) as JC Wyatt, a six-figure earning, corporate woman. Her life is turned upside down when she inherits a toddler after the abrupt death of some long lost cousins. Now, I know most of us didn't become single parents like this, but we all can testify of experiencing the overwhelming fear, denial and dread at realizing you are now a single parent. I love the moment in the movie when JC is still trying to hold on to her carefree, corporate lifestyle (a fantasy), but only becomes more frustrated while trying to hold on to it. She finally retreats, not defeated, but switches gears to adjust to single parenting.

During your single parent transition, you have to stop wanting what you don't have any more or don't have just yet. Focus on the good stuff, the real things and positive people in your life—*right now.* The present is a gift to enjoy today. Get the good in, while you're in the "meantime" phase of your life. Make it all count because it ALL does matter—sooner or later. Make every lesson, a lesson learned.

Don't covet what others have, instead create your own definition of a successful single parent lifestyle. The fallacy of "keeping up with the Joneses" is a serious trap some single parents get caught up in. Most single parents cannot afford to "compete" with the lifestyle of a two-income household. So why try? Once you snapback from the fantasy, you will "see the forest for the tree". The grass *will* look greener on *your* side, but *you've* got to see *and* believe it, for yourself.

It's time to snap out of your single parent fantasy!

Single Parent Fear

Coming From Where I'm From: My greatest moment of fear as a single parent was during the last visit when I took my kids to go see their father. As I backed the car away from where he was standing, tears began to roll down my face. These were tears of release <u>and</u> revelation; but also tears of fear of the unknown journey I was about to begin as a single parent of three kids. Now, I've always ministered to myself with music. At this particular time I had the Yolanda Adams cd cued up and playing "The Battle is the Lord's". Little did I know that the words to this song were setting the stage for the next few years to come.

My Truth/Turning Point: There are many times that as a single parent you will have to reach deep down into your soul to find the courage to keep on moving—through the fear, despite the doubt and beyond the betrayal. And that's just to make it to *tomorrow*! But no matter your situation, one thing rings true. You are not the first, nor will you be the last single parent to persevere. Yes, you will experience moments of paralyzing fear where you tell your body to move . . . and it won't. But it is in those moments that you take a deep breath, wipe the tears away, and begin to take that first *baby* step. As you creep (or even crawl along) you look up in disbelief. No, you're not dreaming. Yes, you are moving, slowly but surely. Next, you pat yourself down to make sure you are still here and standing (as your heart beats a mile a minute). Now, since you *are* still standing, you look straight ahead, eyes zoned in on the target and prepare yourself for that leap of faith!

On your mark! Get ready! Set . . . GO! Do it through the fear! Do it alone! Do it . . . right now!

*Are you dealing with fear? Is it causing you to live in "single parent paralysis"—not able to get up and move on? If so, contact me at **april@ singleparentliving.net** to start your journey from fear to fast forward today!*

Single parent paralysis is NOT an option. Forget the fear and move forward!

Single Parent Finances

Coming From Where I'm From: There are 3 things I will invest in without hesitation: 1) the basics—food, shelter and transportation, 2) a quality education and 3) a healthy lifestyle. You "rule the roost" (as my grandmother used to say). You determine what you spend the money on. You decide when to *spend* it and/or how to *save* it. The key to having more money is to think long-term vs. in-the-moment. A savings account is for you to deposit money—to *save*. A 401K or other retirement funds are set aside for your retirement. A credit card is a tool to *build* your credit not to create debt.

My Truth/Turning Point: As I write this book I have children at three levels of education: elementary (Caleb, 2nd grade), middle (Nyah, 6th grade) and high school (Zaria, 9th grade). I can save money on girl's clothes since my oldest are girls and are only two years apart. I just have to bite the bullet on my son's clothes but that still doesn't mean he gets an exclusive wardrobe makeover every season either. When I shop, I shop for quality clothes—that doesn't automatically mean name brand clothes only. I have always tried to set aside money for my kids to attend college. My kids know they WILL go to college. I know that; they know that. Just as I always knew I would go to "somebody's" college, the same rule applies to my children. So, with every financial decision I make, I consider its impact on their educational well-being. I *try* not to buy items that really don't serve a long-term purpose. Purchases such as a $200 pair of shoes because they are *cute* makes no sense. But I *will* splurge on a $120 pair of running shoes for my daughter Zaria who is a member of an award winning marching band. This purchase ensures her safety as she practices 2-3 times a week and ultimately prevents a hospital visit for injury to her ankles or feet.

Now, single parents, let me keep it real for a minute. Shortly after my divorce and when money was running out really fast, I committed a few financial "no-no's". I cashed out a 401K in order to pay off my car. After seeking advice from a business mentor of mine, he suggested I consider it as an option. With a "long-term" mindset I paid off the car as well as set aside money to pay the penalties in taxes; in the short-term I wouldn't still be burdened with a hefty monthly car note and it helped increase my credit score, showing less debt. Now, a 2nd financial "no-no" that I committed was I paid for a vacation mostly using a credit card. It had been SO long since my family had some fun. Every single parent faces this guilt, don't you? So I gave in to the temptation and splurged for a spring break vacation. While considering how to get the "biggest bang for the buck" we agreed on a 4-day staycation. To save even more money, we traveled by train and planned a nearly non-stop, power-packed, wonder-filled vacation. We literally explored the city right up to the final minute. While waiting on the train to arrive, we hiked by foot to enjoy one last tour spot. Two other tips that added value to our spring break success was to: 1) contact family and friends to let them know you are coming. This could help save money in lodging and food, plus they know all the in's and out's of the area and 2) contact the city's travel and tourism department. That's what they're there for. They will send you a travel packet and be glad to assist in your planning both before and during the trip. It's like having your very own personal vacation planner.

Single parent finances don't have to be a burden if you plan in advance!

Single Parent Guilt—Get a New Attitude

Coming From Where I'm From: Regardless of the circumstances that brought you to your single parent status, the fact still remains—you <u>are</u> a single parent (at least for now). So, with that fact established, it's time to move on. After becoming a single parent, for many years I would beat myself up for not being able to provide for my family as I once had. But one Saturday after wasting nearly a full tank of gas chauffeuring my children around town from one event, dance class, or practice to another, I was totally exhausted! I was running on fumes (literally) trying to maintain a two-income lifestyle on a single parent budget. Something had to give because the guilt (and ripping & running) was killing me!

My Truth/Turning Point: The truth, is you've got to get over the guilt and get a new attitude. No, things aren't like they used to be. Duh, you're living off of one income now. Umm, you are pulling <u>double</u> parent duty, all by yourself, all day, every day. Yes, things are different. But just because things are different, doesn't mean it has to be difficult. **Get over the guilt**. No, it may not be *your* fault that you're a single parent—divorce, loss of a mate, etc. But even *if* your actions did result in you being a single parent, the point of it all is it's still your responsibility to raise your kids responsibly. So, **get over the guilt** and get on with it. Stop being stuck on the "good ole days" and get a new attitude. Your tomorrow (or next month, next year, etc.) can be so much better than your yesterday (or *last* month, *last* year, etc.). But it starts with getting a new attitude. I'm reminded of the lyrics to Patti LaBelle's song "New Attitude". Each time I hear it I want to jump up out of my seat! This should be every single parent's anthem as they break free from the guilt, condemnation and bondage of others and society that sometimes is associated with single parenting. As a single parent, you cannot afford to internalize and self-inflict these oppressive feelings upon yourself, in the form of guilt. It's time to get a new attitude! But it's up to you. Are you ready?

*Are you dealing with single parent guilt? Is it hard for you to "get over it? If so, contact me at **april@singleparentliving.net** to start your journey from guilt to guilt-free single parent living.*

Look into your soul and get a new attitude!

Single Parent Health

Coming From Where I'm From: The past few years have wreaked havoc on my body. I mean, you know it's bad when you spend Mother's Day weekend in the ICU ward. The toll of the years of stress, ripping & running, and little to no "down time" caused my body to finally shut down, literally.

My Truth/Turning Point: I couldn't breathe. Now, I had grown up experiencing sporadic episodes of asthma attacks, so I thought nothing of this shortness of breath until I was literally gasping for air. To this day, I can't explain what came over me. In the previous weeks leading up to this episode, I could've run a marathon (ok, not really, but you know what I mean). But at this very moment, the shortness of breath and excruciating chest pain was telling a whole different story. My mother rushed me to the emergency room. Once admitted, the doctors couldn't determine what was wrong with me. Uh, not a good sign. An IV was started. Multiple vials of blood work was drawn. Repeated EKG's and a cat scan or two. Finally, it was determined—a blood clot and fluid around my heart and lungs. What the what?! I was suffering from a PE. No, I wasn't evading a workout at the gym. I had a Pulmonary Embolism (PE). I'll let you medical geeks look that up. At this point, the specialists finally diagnosed me with having Lupus—an autoimmune disease that primarily affects African-American women. I spent a week in the hospital before I was released. Only to suffer yet another flare up, resulting in spending nearly another week in the ICU ward. My mind was spinning as I was taking into account the amount of money I would be billed for all this extensive care. But I also knew I could not afford to stress out—which I knew was one of the main culprits of my current health crisis. I call my health scare a "crisis" because it was just that. I seriously almost died—twice, within a one month time frame. Through it all, my kids were troopers, my soldiers of love. My posse was ever present, rallying around me during my recovery. Most of all, my Mom maintained her "Queen of Keep-It-Together" status. A couple of times I caught her quietly leaving my room, only to return with saddened, puffy and red eyes from shedding tears. I know she wanted to do more; but what more could she do than continue to be my "Rock of Gibraltar"? Shortly after being released, I vowed to take better care of myself. I mean, it's not like I was a chain smoker or stone cold alcoholic or junkie. But I knew whatever I had to do, I had to do, because if I died, my 60+ year old mother would have to raise my 3 children, alone. Even on a good day, sometimes I can barely handle the responsibility as a 43-year old, so I would not want to burden my own mother with that responsibility. So, in addition to focusing on my health, I also made better choices. The #1 rule was if it caused me stress, then it was not for me. If it was negative, it had to go (people, situations, employment opportunities, etc.).

Ultimately, being diagnosed with Lupus meant a serious phase of purging. Purging is good for the soul, and I had no problem with doing this. When I left the hospital, I felt like a drug dealer with all the prescriptions and list of medications. But the key here is that I was no longer in denial about my health. I followed the doctor's instructions religiously. Even though most of my follow up visits are a still blur, I do remember one conversation I had with my Rheumatologist. He told me that the main reason why his patients relapse, is due to two main things: 1) they are stuck in denial that their health is as critical as it is and 2) patients don't take their medication as prescribed. I thought, I don't want to be sitting in your office. I've had my share of "impromptu" trips to the ICU and ongoing doctor's visits to last me a lifetime. I knew I was not in a state of denial. It was clear that it was "do or die" time, literally. I had a master plan to decrease not only the *quantity* of pills I was prescribed (I was popping six different pills at the time) but even more important, to decrease the *dosage* and/or discontinue certain medications, as well.

So, my Mom became my live-in drill sergeant, carefully monitoring my medication. She also served as my chef, making sure I ate ˎ regularly since the Lupus had my weight fluctuating and the meds messed with my appetite. My friends and family became "borderline stalkers" checking up on me on a daily basis. When I went to my first follow up visits with my 5 specialists, they were all amazed at how quickly I snapped back. It's amazing how the responsibility of single parent living can shift your mindset into making your health care THE top priority. I hadn't realized how near death I was when I was admitted to the ICU ward. I mean I felt *bad*, but not *deathly* ill. All of my specialists cautiously encouraged me to make sure I was taking my medication as prescribed; reminding me that the main reason why people relapse is not due to their medical condition, but because they don't take their meds, especially when they are "feeling fine". I ensured them that I was not stuck on stupid. I'm happy to report that I have cut the amount of prescribed medications down to half of what I initially started with. And with nearly every follow up, my dosages have decreased as well. As a single parent, your health is priority.

Many times when people think about their health, they forget about the *legal* side of health care. Somewhere in between all of my ICU episodes, I made the time to create a power of attorney, medical directive and renewed my will. This is not being morbid, but mindful of taking care of your business. If you don't do it, who will? If not now, then when? Sometimes tomorrow never comes. Even though these legal documents are in place, no one is going to raise your children like you, but at least it gives you peace of mind. When all is said and done, here's the deal—you are a single parent, a mother, and the only parental provider for your kids. So, you've got to be healthy enough to take care of them. As a single parent, you must take care of yourself. YOU are worth it and your kids depend on it, too.

Health care is *every* single parent's #1 priority!

Single Parent Home (Gatekeeper)

Coming From Where I'm From: As single parents your role also *is* that of Primary Gatekeeper. Picture a house with a fence *around* it; with the gate closed in *front* of the house. The fence represents the protective barrier that surrounds the house; whereas the gate represents the guarded, limited access to the house and to those who live there—especially the children.

My Truth/Turning Point: My soul aches with every news report of yet another account of a child being neglected, abused, or killed **in their own home;** even worse, at the hands of **their own** parent(s), their parent's boyfriend or even in the absence of their parent. After grieving over the pain endured by the child, I would think about what my mom did *and didn't do* to protect me as the Gatekeeper of our home. I know first and foremost, she prayed for my safety, especially once I left the comfort of her arms to where my well-being was in the hands of the world—at school, at the mall, movies, skating rink, etc. One main protective measure my Mom abided by was that she never had random men running in and out of our home. Even when she dated, I was not immediately, *if ever,* introduced to those men. When my mom had a date, it was "time to spend the night at grandma's" so I would not meet her male friends. Now think for a moment how awkward and confusing it would be if every other weekend or each month a child got introduced to yet another man, <u>especially</u> if that child is a "fatherless child" (has limited or no contact with their father or a father figure). The man doesn't need the pressure. Neither do you, because you have to respond to the fifty million questions that you know every little kid has. Now who needs that added stress? I know this may seem a bit extreme, but it *automatically* eliminates the mess. Why would you want to introduce that into your home with all that you're already dealing with? See, stuff like that makes single parenting harder than it has to be. Keep in mind that, <u>you</u> are setting the example for the "rules of dating" for your child—your daughter and/or your son. They are always watching and learning from what you do and don't do.

When it came to finding a babysitter, the <u>only</u> available choices were immediate family (my grandparents and aunt) and close friends of my mother. If my mother couldn't get a babysitter, then she didn't get to go out. Plain and simple! I know that's not what you want to hear, but let's think this through for a minute. What—or should I say "who"—is important here? You getting your groove on *OR* your children being safe in their own home? Now, no I'm not saying that every single parent should live like a monk and have no fun. What I <u>*am*</u> saying is that far too many parents are "kicking their kids to the curb" as they party in the club, leaving their children defenseless, like a lamb to the slaughter. Single parents are the Gatekeeper. You <u>must</u> protect your children.

Another key rule in our home was no "unlimited" sleepovers—either at our home and *especially* if at someone else's home. I can count on one hand the number of sleepovers I had and/or went to as a child. And the only time I had a sleepover at my house was for my birthday. The only *recurring* sleepovers I can recall were at a grade school friend's home. You wanna know why? Her mother was a high school friend of *my* mother's (and also was a single parent), so they went *way* back. So, I knew at least on Friday nights when I wanted to go skating, I was already authorized to pack an overnight bag to sleep over. My Mom knew that her friend's house was a safe house (literally). On the flip side of things, I remember when I told my mom about a "weird feeling" I had about one of my school mate's father "looking at me" during a sleepover for her birthday. I'm sure that further fueled the fire of my mother's protectiveness; and rightly so. Lo and behold, years later it was discovered that the father was molesting his daughters. Single parents, YOU are the Gatekeepers for your children. If YOU don't protect them, then who will? If their home is not their safe haven, then where is?

*Not quite sure how to become the Primary Gatekeeper of your home? Contact me for coaching or mentoring at **april@singleparentliving.net**.*

You MUST honor your single parent role as the Primary Gatekeeper.

Single Parent Hustle

Coming From Where I'm From: I'm convinced that a single parent invented the word "hustle" because we are the master of making money or finding ways to make a way out of no way if and when we need to. We will teach, train, write, sing, bake, coordinate and plan at the drop of a dime. In my case, I've always had at least one side hustle to help pay the bills. Most gigs were online or entrepreneurial pursuits which allowed me the freedom and flexibility to still "be there" for my kids.

My Truth/Turning Point: When money began to run out, I knew something had to give. The first things to go were the dance lessons and Saturday afternoon art classes at the art gallery. Well, actually the first thing to go was the **fantasy** that we could continue to do the same things like we were still a two-income family. So, once I snapped back to reality, I began to look for areas where I could add more "pennies to the pot" to pay the bills. I have taught non-credit classes at local colleges. I have graded papers of high school seniors as an online scorer. I have worked the polls (no, not at a strip club) but at voting sites for elections. I have been a mystery shopper. Recently, I became a certified substitute teacher in multiple school districts. So, don't count yourself short, just because you are a single parent. You cannot fall into the trap of thinking you can't do any better. You cannot afford ***not*** to push yourself to the limit—within reason. Understand that it is ***because*** you are a single parent that you have developed a goldmine of "natural" talents and "real life" experience/skills for a job or career you may not have even considered.

Let's take a moment and reflect on all the side jobs you may have "unofficially" held over the years as a single parent. Your many "unwritten roles" as a single parent probably include: gate keeper/security, mind regulator/psychologist, financial planner, motivational speaker, mastermind, teacher, Jackie/Jack-of-all-trades, intercessor/prayer warrior, drill sergeant, boss, advisor/counselor, ruler, mind reader, blocker/defender, shot caller, private investigator, psychiatrist, pharmacist, mentor, cheer leader, goal setter, scientist, mathematician, reading specialist, fashion consultant, event planner, banker, interrogator, preacher, know-it-all, leader, waiter, chauffeur, manager, researcher, confidante, vigilante, youth director, etc. Do you identify with *any* of these roles? I bet you do. The list could go on and on. The point I'm getting at is NOT to discount your single parent experience. You **_do_** have skills. Why? Because you're a single parent!

As a single parent, you learn to master basic skills of everyday living (see the above roles). So, depending on the job you are seeking, the roles listed above are just a few "real life" experiences and skills that could be used as <u>valid</u> experience on a job application. It's all in how you write it on your resume.

If you decide to get your hustle on, the most important thing to remember is to keep your work/life balance in check. Only take a side job IF you can add income <u>while</u> still being there for my children. *The extra money doesn't matter if it's causing mayhem in your home.* In fact, it defeats the whole purpose of starting a side hustle. For example, while a college instructor, I made sure I taught my classes on weekdays—freeing up my weekends for family time. If I did teach a weekend class, it wasn't *every* weekend or it didn't conflict with my children's schedule. While an online scorer, I worked from home and scheduled myself during night hours or when the kids were at school. As a voting site worker, I worked only when there was an election. As a mystery shopper, once again, this multiple stream of income allowed me the freedom to schedule my own hours plus get paid shopping for things I needed (and wanted)—steak dinners, groceries, oil changes, clothes, etc.

*You got skills? Let me create a "real life" resume for you. Are you ready to get your hustle on? Let me coach you on successfully starting or finding a side hustle that pays off. Contact April at **april@singleparentliving.net** to get started today or to register for one of her **"Single Parent Hustle"** webinars.*

Jumpstart the single parent hustle in you!

Single Parent Intuition

Coming From Where I'm From: We've all been there. You're waiting
for your child's name to be called while at the doctor's or dentist's
office. You've just settled in and found an interesting article about your
favorite celebrity or TV show. Or you just found a short, yet senseless
survey that promises to reveal whether you're a perfect parent or not.
So, you get comfortable as you enter into your state of oblivion.
You've selected the perfect seat where no one will bug you or you sit
far enough from a squirming toddler. It never fails, right when you're
halfway through the article, your child's name is called by the nurse.
Convinced that the quiz or article your reading is now on your top
10 list of things to do today; without even looking up, you ask THE
question, "Do you want me to go in with you, honey?" You hold your
breath while secretly hoping your child will say "No", but they say "Yes"
and patiently wait for you to get up.

My Truth/Turning Point: You know where I'm going with this.
You reluctantly rise up, setting a new world record for the amount
of time it takes for your butt to not be in contact with the chair. But
then you catch a glimpse of your child's face. It's not a look of fear,
but of "I need you right now." You can't explain it, but as your child
grabs your hand as you *both* walk towards the room, you just know
that you know that you need to be there with them. That's called
intuition. Intuition kicks in at those times when you can't explain
the feeling, but simply are obedient to it. As a single parent, intuition
is even more important because your "parent radar" is on high alert

24/7/365, sometimes going into overload, causing your level of sensibility and reasoning to be skewed. So, you must <u>never</u> second guess that "gnawing feeling in your gut". It's there for a reason.

Now, I'm going to share a very private story with you. When I was a teenager, I was hanging out with extended family members and neighborhood friends. I think it was a Friday night and it was getting late. My mother let me hang out a little later than usual because I was *with neighborhood friends and family members*—a supposedly safe environment, right? But at about 1:00 am, my mom's single parent intuition told her to get up and go get me, NOW. She was obedient to that "gut feeling" and it saved me from a possible rape. To this day, I am still haunted by the near fatal encounter of what *might* have happened to me that summer night. Single parent intuition is real! It could possibly be life-saving and can be life-changing.

Honor your Single Parent Intuition. That's what it's made for!

Single Parent Job Search

Coming From Where I'm From: Your job search actually begins at the point of even deciding whether to even apply for a particular job or not. When actively job searching as a single parent, you must consider all the "other variables", work conditions and always read the fine print. Yes, you must think through the pros and cons, not *when* you get the job, but *BEFORE* you even apply for it. My mother was a teacher, so I was fortunate that she didn't work long hours and was off when I was off. But here's some advice for those single parents who <u>have</u> to be on the grind to pay the bills.

My Truth/Turning Point: Once again, I say the one key factor to work/life balance as a single parent is being able to BE there for your children. I've been in jobs that had me sacrificing my family time, my health, my sanity all in the name of making more money. In the long run, I was the one losing the most priceless things—family time, perfect health and my peace of mind. For one particular job, I returned to the industry because I was desperate for a job change. But what I didn't realize is that things had changed since I last worked in this job field. When I was in this same position years ago, work relations were different. Nowadays, workplaces are more cutthroat and many (not all) bosses just don't care. They will work you to the bone all the while focused on the bottom line. After many late nights, repeated mandatory weekends, and extended work shifts, I prayed "something has got to give!" Through it all, I never decreased my productivity nor negatively impacted the moral of my department.

As a matter of fact, during that waiting period, I built my skills _and_ my resume, instead of just doing enough to get by (which is an option too many single parents choose). I believe that if you're going to stay at a job, then make the time worth it. Finally, the Lord heard my silent plea and I was released from that demanding job. My reputation was impeccable, my team was producing at record levels, and many people were in awe of "how did she do it?" For more guidance on dealing with bad bosses or surviving toxic workplaces, get a copy of my book *"Good Bosses Gone Bad: How to Survive the Workplace When Your Boss Sucks"* available at **www. GoodBossesGoneBad.com.**

Since then, I have vowed not to get stuck in a workplace rut ever again. I offer the following advice when seeking employment (whether online or outside the home). Take your time when considering the "perfect position". Always read the fine line of every job description because companies have come up with creative job titles that really don't mean a thing. If it says "flexible work schedule", make sure during your job interview that you ask specific questions about it. If the job description lists the expected duties and tasks, ask what percentage you will be required/expected to complete on a given day, weekly, and/or on a quarterly basis. If it says "Monday-Friday, no weekends", verify if there will be *occasional* weekend hours. If so, will they be rotational, mandatory or volunteer. You've got to know *going in* what you're getting yourself into. Ask questions. Be proactive. Once you sign on the dotted line, you're "stuck like Chuck" and employers know this. Sure you can be a no-show or walk off the job saying "take this job and shove it!" But if you walk away from the job or perform poorly, that becomes a permanent record of your job history. You may *think* it won't follow you, but it will. Always remember the saying "Don't burn any bridges." People know people, especially if they work in the same industry or company. You'll still have to explain a job lapse (if you don't include it on your application/resume). Or you will cause a red flag due to your frequent "job hopping". Either way, there's a "paper" or "people" trail that will follow you. So, think about the big picture even <u>before</u> you apply for a new job.

Another solution to your single parent job search is to search for <u>legitimate</u> online jobs. Yes, you must maneuver through the mess, but they *do* exist. Since 2004, I have successfully applied and accepted employment for numerous online jobs.

*Have you thought about becoming a mystery shopper, but don't know where or how to begin? Are you having trouble trying to survive working in a toxic workplace? Let me coach you on finding legitimate online jobs or how to handle a good boss gone bad. Contact me at **april@ singleparentliving.net** to schedule your first coaching session or to register for one of my **"Single Parent Hustle"** webinars.*

Take your time during your next job search. It <u>does</u> matter!

Single Parent Legacy

Coming From Where I'm From: I am a product of a single parent home. I vowed that if God blessed me with my own children, that they would not have to endure the shame, stigma, and daunting circumstances that single children encounter. Yet, here I am—a single parent raising three children. The only difference between myself and my children is that I was a fatherless daughter *since conception.* My three children at least know what it feels like to have a father. Single parenting is hard, but it's not impossible. What legacy do you want to leave for your children?

My Truth/Turning Point: So, how do you break the single parent cycle? What is a single parent to do? For starters, you must have a fierce dedication to sacrifice, by any means necessary. Mentoring is key—for you *and* your children. Operate using a "motivated mindset", because times will get hard. Most pressing is the need to possess a "focused determination" to expose your child to other lifestyles, careers, etc. that they never thought existed or thought were possible for them to pursue. You must take them beyond the four blocks of the neighborhood.

As a single parent, realize that you have been tasked with the most awesome job in the world-raising a child. First and foremost, you must view this as your primary role in life, until your child becomes an adult. Up to that point, your focal point in life is to effectively assist and constantly guide your child for a career in an ever changing workforce and for the world that lies ahead of them. If you do it "right", you will see a shift in roles, where you no longer are the primary decision maker in your child's life. As your child begins to make calculated choices about their future, you then become more of a mentor, on an "as needed" basis. It's like with any goal you set. You don't automatically wake up one day and see you have achieved it. No, there was much planning and ground work done in the initial stages. When there is proper planning, brainstorming, strategizing, etc. then the road to success will yield a huge return on investment. If not, the road will be filled with distractions, potholes and pitfalls that further deter your child from their chosen path time and time again. So, as a single parent you must ask and define for yourself "What is my purpose in parenting?" "What can I do *now*, to see the positive outcome of the fruits of my labor and sacrifice for my child *later?*" "Have I truly fulfilled my role in raising my child?" Regardless of your answer, the "proof is in the pudding." Yes, only time will tell, but what will it say? Train your children not to settle for less. Don't entertain the mess. Stop adding to or allowing stress in your home. As a single parent, YOU must "rule your roost!" If the way you're "ruling" or raising your child isn't right, then make it right today! If not today, then when (tomorrow is not promised to anyone)? If not you (the parent), then who—the streets, drugs, senseless media/ TV/music? As the saying goes "Time waits for no man (or woman)." No one said single parenting would be easy. But I AM here to tell you it doesn't have to be as hard as you make it. I love this quote I came across earlier this year: "Comfortable is not acceptable if you're trying to be exceptional." When you look back at the time that you invested in raising your child, will it show your sacrifice or your selfishness? Will all your years of "sweat equity" show prospects for promise for your child or potential pitfalls and potholes for their future? Now is the time to choose to build a foundation for a future legacy of "more than enough" instead of a legacy of "lag and lack" for your child. With every decision you make, ask yourself "Will this make the current situation better or will it still be the same-ole, same-ole?" Legacy building doesn't just let things be. It pushes beyond what you currently see, feel, and think and propels your level of thinking to operate in a future mode—forecasting the results for 10, 20, even 30 years from now. Legacy building forces you to operate from a mindset where your sense of purpose is driven from your past, present *and* your future. Clarity is key in order for legacy to be possible.

What will your single parent legacy be?

Single Parent Loneliness

Coming From Where I'm From: With each passing year of my single parent status, it gets a little easier to "bite the bullet" and celebrate holidays, birthdays, and special events without a mate. But regardless of the event—Christmas and Valentine's Day are still the kickers!

My Truth/Turning Point: Christmas Day: I remember like it was yesterday. I was out shopping and saw the perfect gift for my son. So, I bought it not realizing that on Christmas day I'd have to assemble the darn thing. OMG! That was the most frustrating Christmas ever, where for a split second I secretly wished my ex was there. But, as single parents, you have to be careful NOT to open doors that have been closed. You must never forget, even in your most weakest moment, that they were closed for a reason.

Valentine's Day: No other day illuminates single parent loneliness than Valentine's Day. I'm just being honest. And since we're being so honest, as single parents (more so for single moms) you MUST be aware of men that prey on you and the marketing industry that exploits your emotions at this time of the year. For the past few years, I've vowed to subtly disconnect from media and men around this time. Why? The temptation is too great! "Love" commercials are broadcasted 24/7, everywhere—TV, radio, online, even billboards on the highways. Covert, calculating, yet suggestive texts, phone calls, emails and online posts start to increase, especially late at night. Single moms, realize that this is a "grooming phase" that you must

<u>not</u> succumb to. Now, ladies here's a general rule to live by that'll save you from an embarrassing booty call. If he hasn't said to you what he needed to say to you *before* 9:00 pm, then it can wait until *after* 9:00 am tomorrow morning. I'm just keeping it real.

Do you want to know my simple solution to combating single parent loneliness? Get selfish! I know it's hard to be selfish when you are a single parent, but darnit, it's just ONE day! Now, let me clarify. When I say "selfish" I don't mean go overboard. What I DO mean, is take a day (or two) and go ahead and do the darn thing—get a manicure AND a pedicure, book a massage AND a facial, take in a dinner AND a movie. Now, in the case of Valentine's Day, who says you *have* to celebrate it ON the 14th. Remember, as a single parent, you make our own rules! You don't have to answer to anyone, but yourself. This instance is no different. But the key is to have your day *before* or *after* Valentine's Day; ***never*** the day of or that weekend. That would be single parent suicide! You MUST steer clear of the couples that are coming out of the woodwork to celebrate their love. I'm not hating, I'm just being real. Practice the "duck-and-weave" principle during Valentine's Day to avoid seeing the "hourly" flower deliveries at work, or hearing the sappy extended "I-miss-you-too" phone calls of your coworkers, etc. Hey, it's a matter of survival of the single parent. I'm not hating, I'm just being real. And yes, I encourage you to round up your "single parent posse" and really get it in! Bum rush that restaurant ya'll been talking about hitting up. Take in that movie you've been trying to catch since you missed the premiere weekend release. Whatever adventure you and/or your posse decide, keep it positive—no male bashing allowed!

Single Parent Loneliness doesn't <u>always</u> have to be a part of your single parent living.

Single Parent Mindset

Coming From Where I'm From: After my divorce I really struggled with the fact that I was now "one of them"—a single parent. I know for some of you readers that sounds strange. Yes, the ink was dry on the divorce decree. Yes, my husband and I had been separated for years prior to the divorce. But for SO long, I had been a wife, mother, part of a "perfect couple"; but now after my world had crashed, I had to pick up the pieces and adjust my lifestyle, radically. I needed a minute to wrap my mind around this shift to single parenting.

My Truth/Turning Point: Who better to turn to for advice than my mother, who at the time was married, but for most of my childhood was my sole provider, i.e. a single parent. One afternoon, during my divorce phase, she and I had one of our candid "Now what?" discussions. She said "April, it's not your fault. Understand that it <u>will</u> be hard, but you can do it. I only had one child—you. You have three. But you're not the first single parent to be abandoned by their husband with three kids, and you won't be the last." I realized that my mother's words were words of wisdom and truth—I knew I had to "handle it" because the truth hurts but more importantly, it sets you free. So, as single parents you do what you do best every day—"hunker down" in the trenches and get on with the business at hand—single parenting. I'm not saying it won't be scary, exhausting and sometimes confusing. Honestly, for most of the first few years as a single parent, I "did it" with much fear, many tears and few cheers. But today, I am fearless (ok, most days), tears are few and far in between, and cheers of encouragement come more often than before. A crucial factor in my single parent snapback phase was searching my soul in an attempt to get my swag back. I know it may sound vain, but that essentially was the catalyst to my change in mindset. If any change was gonna come, it has to begin with you. If you are going to be a better *parent*, it has to begin with you being a better *person*—to yourself, first and foremost. If your environment was going to be more positive, you have to be positive in your thoughts, words and actions. You then have to be committed to the change at hand. As a single parent, there is little to no time for error. No, it's not fair; but it is what it is. And in knowing and accepting this, you move on and move forward, from this day on. No turning back in fear. No looking back in regret. Only keeping your eyes on the prize. Determined not to let any further dreams go deferred. With a made up mind, move and operate on a whole new level of being, doing and thinking. It's already there within you—the soul of a single parent. Tap into it. Embrace it. Welcome it. Walk with it as it leads and guides you on your single parent journey. Enjoy the ride!

*Are you wondering "Where do I go from here?" Let me coach you on successfully searching your soul to determine the next step of your single parent journey. Get started today by contacting me at **april@ singleparentliving.net**!*

It's time to snapback and get your SWAG on!

Family Pictures

April & Zaria

April & Nyah

April & Caleb

Boyd-Noronha Family

Photos courtesy of Nelson's Photo & Video Productions

Single Parent . . . Moms
Raising Daughter(s)

Coming From Where I'm From: I thank God that he blessed me with two daughters. As a single mom, I am conscious of my role to live my life as an example for them. I realize that the way I respond to a man, most likely will be the way *they* respond to a boy/man. I am  constantly challenged with balancing the act of being a "strong black woman" vs. simply *being a woman.* I am conscious of the "traditional" mother role, while sustaining a household alone—being the mother and the father. I am careful to keep my thoughts, words and actions positive—especially when talking about my children's father and men in general. As a divorced woman, I need to make sure they know that not *all* men are "bad" and that not *all* relationships end badly. Equally important is the need for them to grasp the fact that all outcomes and consequences—good and bad—stem from choices you make (or don't make), early one.

My Truth/Turning Point: As a single parent, the roles of a mother and a father become blurred. The single parent role plays "double time" at *all* times; whereas in a two-parent household each parent has the luxury to "tag team" and assume a particular role (ex. nurturer, discipliner, provider, protector, etc.). But in a single parent household, the single parent must be *all* roles to *each* child at *ALL* times. This is a hard (darn near impossible) thing to do—every single day! My daughters are fortunate in that they have great memories of bonding with their father when they were younger—fishing, vacations, swimming, grand birthday parties, elaborately decorated bedrooms, hugs and kisses, etc. He was a great provider and father.

I encourage all single parent moms to be THE example of a "real woman" for their daughters. I am determined to be a mom/woman/ friend (even BFF) that my daughters admire and can confide in. Now, I understand that some single moms never had a positive *female* figure in their own life. So you are faced with having to create an environment that honors the essence of a woman, while searching and striving within *yourself* to be the woman _you_ want to be.

How in the world do you do that? One great example is described in the Bible in Proverbs 31: 10-31 (NIV). Which describes the characteristics of a "virtuous woman". Simply put, a virtuous woman is a woman who is "about it." She is focused, smart, determined, fierce, financially savvy, giving, secure and always on the grind (making a dollar out of fifty cents). She handles her business.

Another main concern, just as it was for my mother, is that my girls not be taken advantage of—mentally and physically for the most part. Since becoming a single parent and after I got *my* mind right; I began to have candid, yet age appropriate discussions with my daughters about life, goals, virtues, boys, men, etc. My daughters know that at any given moment, I will call a "no holds bar" Q & A session with them. They know at these sessions that *any* topic is open for discussion (yes, any topic, including my "relationship" with their father). As they get older, many times *they* will call the meeting. It is at these times that I stop what I am doing and we talk. Sometimes we vent and get raw with our emotions, other times we just reminisce about "the good ole days" when money was over flowing and life seemed so carefree. But, the point of these meetings is to build trust and an open relationship where they feel comfortable enough to come to me—not their friends, not the school counselor, not the youth director at church—ME! My daughters know I will tell them the truth, nothing but the truth, so help me God (and I don't have to hold my hand on a Bible in a court of law). They know, "Mommy's word is bond!" And that's how it should be.

Single moms raising daughters is difficult, but do-able!

Single Parent . . . Moms Raising Son(s)

Coming From Where I'm From: My son looks just like his father—he's so cute. But I have to remember that he also has his own identity. On a daily basis I battle with the fact that when I look into my son's eyes, I cannot penalize him for his father's actions, especially since  he's a mini version of him. On a stressful day, I struggle to keep my words positive in regards to my children's father. It's a struggle that by the grace of God, gets a little bit easier each day.

My Truth/Turning Point: The truth is I'm a good mother, but I don't know how to raise my son. I don't know how to tie a tie. I did not potty train my son. At that stage, I was at a point in my life where I just couldn't do it. Mommy Confession: I never taught my son how to pee standing upright, to this day I don't know how he learned. But I thank God for old school women who picked up the slack at his daycare center. In our home, my son is surrounded by women—me, his grandmother, and his two older sisters. There is no "regular" male interaction <u>at all</u>. In my attempt to make up for this gap, I am "hard" on my son. But "being hard" doesn't replace being a man. I am not a man. I am a woman. I am not a dad. I am a mom. I'm constantly challenged to act like a woman, while trying to train him up to be a man. It's especially challenging since I was not raised by a father figure in my own home. So, I really have <u>no</u> clue! The closest male presence I had in my life while growing up was my grandfather, but he was not my father.

I recently began a one-woman "single parent crusade" to make a conscious effort to engage my son in *any* activities that promote healthy male initiatives—boy scouts, athletic programs (soccer), music lessons (drums) and church programs (Royal Ambassadors). But in addition to establishing a consistent *group* male bonding experience, I am committed to finding suitable males to mentor my son, individually. But before you venture out to shuffling your son in community youth programs, remember consistency is the key factor. You have to be committed to extra time involved in attending every practice, meeting and special event. You have to make sure that any program you enroll your son in is legitimate and reputable. I hear you asking yourself "But how do I do that?" Let your son participate in programs that only other single parents can <u>personally</u> refer you to. Also, ask other single parents their opinion of a program you're considering, especially if their child has already been a participant. Here's the deal. Your son does not need yet another male figure in his life that is hit-or-miss and inconsistent. Your goal is to break the pattern that was started by his father. So, as I looked around my inner circle of family and friends I was faced with the following categories of suitable male role models/mentors:

1) Family members—I am an only child; so there are no uncles. My biological father was never a part of my life. My step-father is deceased; so there are no grandfathers. I have one male cousin but he has no children of his own (it takes a special mindset to be a single parent), plus he deals with his own daily struggles of life not to mention his job requires him to travel sometimes. So no male cousins available, at least on a consistent basis.

2) Male friends—This category is the most challenging— approaching a male in a <u>sincere</u> attempt to join you in **a pact**

(that's what it really is) to be present in your son's life. You're not looking for a fly-by-night or here-today-gone-tomorrow male presence. You don't want to start something and then it ends abruptly, creating yet another void or negative male experience for your son. It will have defeated the purpose and now you're further perpetuating a pattern of "male voidance", not intentionally, but it is what it is. So, when I call this interaction a "pact", I mean it! Know that this involves a serious commitment. Now, here are the rules when it comes to making a pact with male friends, for the sake of your son. First, be <u>very</u> clear that this "special request" is about your son—not you & him hooking up. When you speak about a time to meet, keep it brief and to the point. You don't need to know how each other's day went—this is about the business of bonding with your son, <u>not</u> bonding with you. When you meet for the drop off, meet at a public place; not at each other's home. That's too close for comfort. With this category of males, you have to find the balance between you being a stalker vs. a constant reminder service. By this I mean a level of discretion is needed. I never made a public spectacle about my son meeting with his male mentor. I made sure my son was comfortable and excited about the time spent with the trusted male figure. In addition to that, you must assume the role of a "constant reminder service". Understand that this pact is an *added* service that a male friend is volunteering to do. It is not a requirement, nor is it court-ordered. This is not a part-time job where he is earning any extra income. Honestly, it probably is not as much a priority for him as it is for you and your son. So, keep that in mind as you contact him to arrange mentoring time with your son. You don't want to stalk him, but make sure he remembers to include your son in an activity at least 1-2 times a month. One way to ensure consistency is to <u>initially</u> set up times, dates, and/or days to meet ahead of time. That way it limits confusion and miscommunication in an already awkward arrangement.

Now, because you are a <u>single</u> mom, steer clear of married men *unless* he <u>and his wife</u> offer to spend time with your son. More important, this invitation should be *initiated* by the married couple, <u>not you</u>.

You don't want to get caught up in any blurred lines. Single parenting is already complicated, don't make it any worse by dragging another family into the madness.

3) Church and community groups. This option *should* be the easiest out of the three, but it seems to be the hardest at times. I've found the most success in two categories—younger males (mid 20-s to mid-30's) and the "surrogate grandpas". But even in this pool of men I found some to be out of touch—not sure how to *really* help beyond giving a hi-five while passing by your son or rubbing your son's head like he's a lost little puppy. Or many of the surrogate grandpas are raising their <u>own</u> grandsons, so time and commitment are factors working against their earnest attempt to help you. Even in the church and when dealing with community groups, single moms must be aware of the "fox in sheep clothing" who is sitting next to you in the pew or on the bleachers. Some men appear to be committed to bonding with your son but have misguided intentions to "prey" while in the house of "pray"er. One final note of caution is when a younger male agrees to mentor your son, once again discretion is needed. You know people gossip in church, in your community, anywhere really. You *never* want to appear as if you are dating the male who is mentoring your son. Some people think it's cool to be a cougar, but not in this case. Remember, it is all about your son, not you. When my son and his mentor's paths crossed, I encourage my son to go over and greet his mentor—without me. Now of course we acknowledge each other's presence (from afar) with a smile, nod, and/or a brief "Hey!" but that is it. DISCRETION is necessary! He has a reputation to keep, especially if he's on the market to date. Also, the male mentor must know, at all times, that you are grateful for him choosing to spend time with your son. He must never feel as if he is being used as just a weekend babysitter, male meal ticket, or a pawn for personal daycare services. From time to time, offer to pay for the expenses or gas money for the activities spent with your son. Now, a *real* gentleman will not take money from a single mom, however, a *real* single parent will at least offer, from time to time.

*Do you need help in finding a mentor for your son? Are you interested in starting or joining a local group of moms raising sons? Visit **www.singleparentliving.net** for details.*

Single moms raising sons is serious business!

Single Parent Posse (Support System)

Coming From Where I'm From: As an only child, I've never had a lot of friends. By choice, even as an adult, I *still* don't have many friends. But the few friends that I DO have are my "ride or die" chicks—my posse. Webster defines posse as "a large group often with a common interest". Our code of ethics is "I got you, you just simply need to ask"—that is our common interest.

My Truth/Turning Point: Every single parent needs a posse. While transitioning to my single parent status, my support system consisted of about 4 people, in addition to my mom. Yep, that's it—no entourage, busy bodies, gossip crew, etc. These were my friends that I could call at 3am and just vent—while they listened (or dozed off a few times, but at least they picked up the phone). These were the people who I _knew_ would tell me the "stone cold" truth (even though it would hurt); but I listened because I knew they said it out of love for me and my children. These were the sistas who called to make sure I got out of bed and took a shower that day. Even to the point that they stayed on the phone until they heard the water running. My posse also consisted of one male (my brother from another mother) who always had my back, especially from the safety standpoint. I remember his first bits of advice to me after my divorce was to change the locks on the door. It takes a man to understand the psyche of another man. His support was invaluable because he helped me understand the mindset of a man. Your posse are the friends that suggest you go talk to a therapist because your life is so turned upside down and they don't want you to lose it and possibly harm yourself and/or your kids. Your posse **never** judges you, yet love you, unconditionally, through the pain, tears, heartache and stress. This support system of diehard friends pray for your breakthrough, stand in the gap while you "go through". They also are the first ones to celebrate the success in your journey to snap back and get your swag on. Your posse goes beyond being just your biological family members. Sometimes they are the only family you have or will ever need.

*Are you still struggling to get back up again? Let me help you set up your single parent posse. Email me at **april@singleparentliving.net** to get started today!*

Your single parent posse is critical to successful single parent living!

Single Parent Possible

Coming From Where I'm From: My main motivation is fueled each day when I look into my child's eyes. I see their faith and trust in me that "Mommy's gonna make everything alright!" Little do they know that some days, I don't even have a clue. And most days it feels like I'm living "just enough to get by." But each day I try to answer the call of duty in response to their unconditional love.

My Truth/Turning Point: Because my children believe in me, I am encouraged to be the best parent that I can be. Because I am a single parent, the sole responsibility that sits squarely on my shoulders seems impossible to bear at times. But it is in these moments that I do the one thing that always brings me comfort and clarity—I pray! When I really need guidance on raising my children, no one can provide a surefire point of view like God. Joshua 24:15 says "But as for me and my household, we will serve the Lord." (NIV). Once you are committed and dedicated to your role as a single parent, you can then walk boldly in the promise of God found in Matthew 19:26, "Jesus looked at them and said, "With man this is impossible, but with God **all things are possible**." Now *all* things that you are trying to accomplish <u>must</u> be in alignment with God's Will for you as a single parent. For instance, if you're praying that your cute and sexy new co-worker or neighbor will be your next mate, you've got it all twisted. Your focus should be on your employment, your household and providing for your children—not getting your groove on with somebody new. In order for <u>all</u> things to be possible, your mind must be set on the right priorities—new finances, not a new fiancée; raising a child in a protective environment, not raising the roof in a club every night; creating an environment of encouragement, not of chaos; being there for your children, not somewhere with someone else. If your priorities are in check, then check your doubt at the door. With faith, <u>all</u> things are possible, with God.

*Are you ready to speak possibility to your situation? Let me help take your single parent lifestyle to the next level. Contact me at (816) 214-3717 or email me at **april@singleparentliving.net** to get started today!*

Get ready to speak "possible" into your single parent lifestyle!

Single Parent Prayer

Coming From Where I'm From: Many of my prayers have been silent ones. Most of my prayers have been a simple sigh or a moan from the depth of my soul because I was too stressed and overwhelmed to even put words to what I was feeling at that exact moment. Some of my sincerest prayers stem from being able to forgive those who have hurt and/or hindered me—intentionally or not. I've come to a point in my spiritual life where I automatically ask "Father, forgive them for they don't know what they've been doing" even though I know some of them do. But one simple prayer (or better yet, it's my single parent *plea*) that sums it all up and helps shift the perspective on my current situation is "Lord, something has got to give!"

My Truth/Turning Point: The soul of a single parent can only be comforted through prayer. Prayer *by* the single parent. Prayers *for* the single parent. Prayers *on behalf of* the single parent as others stand in the gap for them. If according to the Bible in James 5:16 (NIV), "The prayer of a righteous person is powerful and effective", then all single parents should be praying fanatics who seek answers, expect blessings but only if you pray, unselfishly, for the right thing/reason! The other key to successful single parent prayer is the timing. When do single parents need to pray? All day, every day—in a perfect world. But in the practical, realistic world the two prime times for single parents to pray are: 1) when you first wake up, before the "ripping and running" of your day begins and 2) right before you go to bed, when your home is quiet and it's just you, all by yourself, in the peace and quiet. Basically, you pray as you begin <u>and</u> end your day. These are the moments where you can get unplugged from the noise and craziness of the world and get plugged back into the peace of God. And it is in these moments of prayer and solitude, where you find the highest level of peace that brings about clarity and serenity. These are two elements that are essential for successful single parent living. I know it may be hard to get a moment to yourself (remember, I have three kids). But know this! Prayer is *the* key to your single parent sanity. Wanna keep it all together? Have a moment of prayer, don't have a pity party! Don't get pissed *off*, instead, get your prayer *on*! Having a bad day? Take a moment to pray. Wanna have it your way? Pray! When things don't go your way . . . pray.

Single parent prayer takes your life to a whole new level of living!

Single Parent Promises

Coming From Where I'm From: Sometimes it's so hard for a single parent to keep their promises when we ourselves have experienced so many broken promises—from our ex, former lover/mate, family, friends, bosses, coworkers, EVERYBODY—including ourselves. But if you *can* be true to anyone else, let it be to your child.

My Truth/Turning Point: Since I have three children, I have to be extremely careful in committing to things. Kids bombard parents so easily and innocently with their sincere requests that sometimes the guilt gets the best of us and you just cave in. But then when reality sets in, you spend more time beating yourself up for saying "Yes!" It's been a long road to get to the point of keeping my promises— not because I'm not a promise keeper, but because it seems as if Murphy's Law hangs out at my home 24/7/365. You know the saying, "If anything can go wrong, it will." So, what is a single parent to do? Keeping this in mind, I've learned never to give an immediate answer to a child's request. It's not to torture them or that you're a procrastinator (well, sometimes it is). But they can wait a minute or two for your final answer. In the meantime, you wrack your brain and sync it up with your e-planner (or better yet, cross reference it with your middle child that has a photogenic memory and is a budding event planner) to ensure there are no overlaps in any events and prior commitments you've already made for yourself and/or the family. If the "coast is clear", make that promise and make every effort to keep it. If there is a conflict, then say so, explain why, then bow out gracefully. Only to begin preparing for the next ambush (sure to come within the next few minutes).

"*I promise*" can be two fatal words of determination or defeat for a single parent.

Single Parent Resilience

Coming From Where I'm From: My current single parent theme song/motto is "So Fresh and So Clean!" by the hip hop duo OutKast. It may not be how I always look on the outside, but I always try to let my little light shine from the inside out. My glow is undeniable and unexplainable. In addition to my theme song, my current ring tone is "Single Life" by Cameo. Oddly enough, it is a daily reminder of my primary role, divine purpose and it keeps me focused.

My Truth/Turning Point: The truth is, many people wonder why I am so comical. I can crack a "gut busting" joke at a moment's notice and have even the most pessimistic of persons smiling from ear to ear. Little do they know, most times I laugh and joke around to keep from crying from the trying times I endure as a single parent. Webster defines resilience as "the ability to become strong, healthy, or successful again after something bad happens; an ability to recover from or adjust easily to misfortune or change." Yep, that pretty much sums up a typical single parent lifestyle. I think single parents are the epitome of resilience because it's an everyday mode of survival. Yes, bad things happen, life is hard at times; yet single parents still manage to rise to the occasion to raise their children and take care of business-time and time again. Now, that's resilience! When you think of characteristics of a single parent, resilience should be one of the top five on your list. Without single parent resilience households will crumble and fold from the pressures of life, goals will remain unreached, dreams will continue to be deferred, valley lows will be a regular dwelling place instead of experiencing pivotal mountaintop moments on a regular basis. With resilience, single parents can beat the odds, be *more* than conquerors, survive the storms of life, make a way out of no way, and tell the naysayers "I told you so!" I see moments of resilience in single parent lives every day. Are you a resilient single parent? Have you "been there and done that" and even have the t-shirt to prove it? If so, be proud of your single parent resilience. It is not an easy thing to do. It takes courage when change is all around you. It takes persistence when procrastination is knocking at your door. It takes a determined mindset when all you wanna do is give up when it gets so hard to press on. But here's the deal. *Now* is the acceptable time for single parents to rise, raise up and regain the respect and honor due for "pressing on" when you could've just let life pass you by. I proudly salute you—single parent!

Single parent resilience is <u>required</u> for successful single parent living!

Single Parent Restoration

Coming From Where I'm From: I am a firm believer in "what comes around, goes around." I also believe that there is a time to sow and a time to *reap* what you sow. So, as I look back over my life and reflect on all the negative things I've had to deal with—the deceit, betrayal, pain, lies, sadness, back stabbing, season of lack, oppression, etc. I can also rejoice in knowing that this too shall pass.

My Truth/Turning Point: Through my single parent journey I've often compared myself to the righteous man named Job in the Bible. Job was a man who God was well pleased. He strived to always do the right thing and God blessed him indeed. But once Satan saw how Job was faithful and blessed abundantly by God, He challenged God by basically asking "Let me see how much he will serve you after all hell breaks loose in his life?" God agreed and the devil got busy. All hell broke loose—the devil attacked Job's family and all his worldly fortunes. Long story short, Job was tempted and tried to the very soul of his being. He lost everything . . . or so it seemed (duh, duh, duhhhh!). The end of the story reminds us of God's faithfulness to His people. His people are everyday people that love and trust in Him completely. Personally, I believe God has a "special place" in his heart for those that care for children—whether your role is a single parent, guardian, teacher, coach, youth director, etc. I rest on the promises of God, that those that honestly and faithfully accept their role as parent, guardian, or caregiver of children will receive restoration for all that was blocked, taken and/or stolen from them. So, when I look to the heavens, from where I know my divine help comes from, I am comforted in knowing that restoration is due—to me *and* my children! And not just restoration of "barely enough" but of "more than enough." Restored finances, relationships, peace, health, serenity, joy, prosperity, a right mind, gainful and purposeful employment, safety and security for you and your family. Whatever was taken from you, it's time to take it back. Reclaim restoration as yours, right now!

It's time to (re)claim your single parent restoration!

Single Parent Sanctuary

Coming From Where I'm From: Even though my home is not my own, per se, it is my little slice of sanctuary. I live in separate quarters in a house that is in my mother's name. It is a big change from where I used to live—home on the corner lot, 3 bedrooms and a loft, 2 ½ bathrooms, 2 car garage. In 2007, I packed up my minivan and moved back home with my three kids. Having been a stay-at-home Mom, I had no job, but I had an MBA and a resume full of community service activities. At that time I was separated from my then husband and was currently living off of the bank accounts that I shared with him (prior to our divorce). In 2008, no more than 3 months later, my stepfather suddenly died after being in a coma. So not only was I experiencing the grief of a marriage gone bad, but now I had to comfort my mother as she grieved the death of her husband. As a single parent, I also had to shoulder the burden of helping my children heal from the hurt of the loss of yet another male figure in their life. First, their father (due to a divorce) and now their grandfather (due to death). Needless to say, a *lot* was going on in our home! So in 2009, my mom and I decided to move to a new home to start a new life—as a widow and divorcée. Sounds like the perfect title to an upcoming Lifetime ® movie, doesn't it?

My Truth/Turning Point: See, while most people feel a need for speed, I've always felt a need for sanctuary, peace and tranquility. On most mornings my daily routine consists of my tea and moments of meditation.

Since they say "home is where the heart is", then please show me some love! Regardless of my residence, my favorite place of sanctuary (otherwise known as my hide out) is the bathroom. I know, it may sound weird. Most of you probably would designate your bedroom as your place of serenity. To that I say, to each his (or her) own. But one thing for sure my kids know, especially my son, that there will be *serious* consequences if they ever bust unannounced into my bathroom.

As a single parent, you must take this sanctuary issue seriously. You've got to have a place, spot, or room to yourself where you can de-stress, relax, release, and let go of the day's mess. Even if you had a good day, your sanctuary is your perfect place to go to reflect on that happy moment and to stay centered on that good feeling.

When watching the movie, "The Wiz", I get all warm and fuzzy inside when Diana Ross begins to sing "When I think of home, I think of a place where . . ." Don't even act like you don't know the song; I know you do! See, not only should your home be a refuge for your children, but for you, the single parent, too. Do you feel the same as the character "Dorothy" in "The Wiz"? Is there a song or memory that just takes you back home when you hear or think about it? That's the power of sanctuary and having a place of serenity.

Single parent sanctuary and serenity is needed for single parent survival!

Single Parent Selfish

Coming From Where I'm From: Be strategically selfish with your time, mind and body. I recently was diagnosed with Lupus—the autoimmune disease that essentially attacks your body when you get sick. It took ending up in the ICU ward on Mother's Day weekend to realize that I had to stop being all things to everyone, i.e. Superwoman, Supermom. It was time for me to do me. To take care of myself, <u>first</u>. I know that sounds extremely selfish. And you know what—IT IS!

My Truth/Turning Point: Think of it like this. If something happens to you, who is going to take care of your kids? It's not a matter of *if* but *when* you run out of steam. So, who is going to be there to pick up the pieces and keep the ball running? As a single parent you know all too well the answer to this question. The responsibility lies squarely on your shoulders—whether you're 100% at your best or simply plugging along on fumes, aimlessly put-putting around. YOU are the single parent. Only YOU can love your children like they are your own because they *are* yours. Your parents can't love them like you—they're the GRANDparents. Your siblings can't love your children like you—that's why they're called aunts and uncles. You get the picture? YOU are called, set apart, destined to be THE parent to your child(ren). You must own up to this reality (if you haven't already). Then and only then will you be able to snapback and get your SWAG on like never before. Now, don't get me wrong. When I encourage you to "be selfish" that does not mean to kick all sensibility and responsibility out the door. As a single parent, you know proper planning and budgeting is key. The only difference, from this point on, is to *strategically* plan some "me time" on a regular basis. For some, a regular basis is every day (30 minutes to 1 hour). For others, their "regular basis" could mean once a week or twice a month. Only you can set a scheduled time to "do you". This "me" mindset has been a life saver, literally. Instead of always going to the movies with the whole family, sometimes I go to the movies by myself or with my friends. Or when I want to treat myself to dinner, instead of going out to eat with the kids, I go by my darn self. I know some of you are shaking your head as you read those two dreadful words "by myself." You're saying to yourself "I can't do that!" Trust me, you can. I do it all the time and I'm starting to see more singles do it, too. But it all boils down to the fact that the most *under*valued person in your life is YOU! Oh yeah, it's time to be selfish. Single parents end up doing everything for everyone else, most times feeling so depleted, that there's little to no energy to then take care of yourself. This scenario plays out over and over again—and no one wins. Actually, the biggest loser is the single parent—you. Correct me if I'm wrong. But you know I'm right. So go ahead and feel no guilt while being selfish. Just in case you're worried about finding the right balance of "single parent selfishness" here's the best indicator. If you take some time to be selfish and afterwards you feel rejuvenated, refreshed and less stressed—then that's a great thing. On the flip side, if you set aside some time to be selfish, but afterwards are consumed with guilt and are <u>still</u> stressed out, then something ain't right. You need to go back to the drawing board and really evaluate *what* you did, *why* you did it, *who* it was done with and *when* (timing is everything). Was your selfish moment done in spite? Did your selfish time end up having you making up more time (playing catch up)? Then you didn't do it right. Understand that single parent selfishness is meant to be a tool to get *ahead*, not set yourself *back*. In order to get the best results it cannot be a random thing. It is a strategic move that takes you one step closer to your single parent serenity and sanity. Strategy and timing are two critical principles needed for to you live a successful single parent lifestyle. As the saying goes, "If momma ain't happy, no one is!" Even more important, if momma ain't healthy, then no one is getting taken care of properly. That's why it is so important to be selfish. So, go ahead and get selfish. If done right, somewhere along the way you'll also find a bit more of happiness, serenity, and a quiet determination to feel like pressing on—despite your current circumstances.

It's time for single parents to be selfish!

Single Parent "Sick & Tired of Being Sick & Tired"

Coming From Where I'm From: For some single parents, the words "stressed", "depleted", "depressed", "fed up" and "exhausted" are synonymous with single parent living. On many days, when asked how I'm doing I want to shout at the top of my lungs "I'm sick and tired of being sick and tired!" Now, when venting to your inner circle or in the privacy of your own home, that's fine to confess. But you can't be so honest in public or around your boss or coworkers—that'll be career suicide. They'll start working on your exit plan or figure out a way to fire your butt faster than you can say "But I was just joking!"

My Truth/Turning Point: Single parents have got to be the biggest fakers out there (and I mean that in a good way). When asked by our children if you're still hungry, you say "No" so they will have enough to eat. When your boss asks if you'd like to pick up extra hours at work, you say "Sure!" knowing that's extra gas money for the week, but less quality time at home with your family. When your child comes home from school asking you for money for a field trip, you say "Here you go!" as you reach into your secret, *me-time* stash. When your child texts you to come pick them up NOW after a late night school event, you get up and reply "Ok, Mommy's on the way"; while fighting the fatigue with every mile driven. But no parent is a Super Parent—no matter how hard you try. So, how do you keep it going without falling apart? You map out the master plan.

With every request made by your children, you have to determine how to get the "biggest bang for the buck." Decide which decision will yield the biggest return for the <u>whole</u> family. By return, I mean you have to weigh the pros & cons of the situation at hand. Timing is a main factor. For instance, calculating the daily amount of gas plus wear & tear on the <u>one</u> vehicle that you have is critical. You must determine, is it better to pay for childcare or have the younger siblings tag along, hoping they won't embarrass the rest of the family at your oldest child's recital or special event. Figuring out how much "uninterrupted" sleep you can fit in on any given night is crucial because you no longer have the luxury of calling in sick. You are a single parent. Can you remember how long it's been since you had a "moment of escape" to connect with yourself? Are you spreading yourself too thin? Does your child *absolutely* have to attend the event they're bugging you about or would a quiet, family night at home be ok? Single parents must have the fortitude to say "No!" to your children then and be ok with it. You can__not__ reneg. Realize that your child's social life won't totally be scarred if they miss this one event. If you're sick and tired of being sick and tired, then just say "No!" This is one of the simplest, yet surefire ways to snap back and claim your life back. Another way is to just slow down. It is so easy for single parents to get caught up in the "ripping and running" routine. But it takes its toll after a while. Your body will shut down (trust me, I know from experience). This is a dangerous state to be in. When you can't go on, then nothing gets done. As a single parent, your goal is to be well rested until the next time you hear your child cry "Mommmmm, can you . . . ?"

Single parents are the biggest givers, too. You give and give, even until the point where it hurts. Now sometimes, this level of sacrifice is needed. But most times, since you are the sole provider of our household, it is essential to reserve your strength for when it really counts. At times, you so easily let others take from you—your money, talents, time, love—until you have no more to share. Well, I'm here to encourage you to fight the cycle of being "sick & tired" and snapback to single parent reality. I must admit this step is rather easy for me since I'm a single child. But, remember all you have to do is be selfish (refer to the previous chapter "Single Parent Selfish").

Yep, that's it. Flip the script and get into selfish mode. Let the De La Soul song from 1989 become your theme song—"Me, Myself, and I." Now, of course you can't use this concept ALL the time. But when you feel a severe case of fatigue and stress coming on after a long day at work or a week of ripping and running—simply sigh and then declare "It's just me, myself, and I!" Then get up, walk to your room (or place of sanctuary) and close your door. The key is to tune out all noise and interference that you're sure to hear from your kids. I know this can be one of the hardest things to do. But think of it this way. It's either solitude or be featured on the next episode of "Snapped" on the Oxygen ® channel. So, I challenge you to set realistic limits and stop faking and giving in to others all the time. More important, listen to your body. Just like a car lets out steam when it is overheated, your body will speak to you when you are overwhelmed. Depending on whether you listen to it or not, it will either respond by shutting down (and you find yourself in the ICU ward) or your body will thank you for taking a "time out" to get it together. As single parents, you are "on guard" 24/7. You need to always be ready to snapback—feeling recharged and ready to move forward. In order to do that, sometimes it'll take a quick power nap in the afternoon. Other times, it'll take you shouting out an unapologetic "NO!" Either way, it's up to you to be proactive in turning your life around. If you're tired of being sick and tired, then make that change, today. How are your eating habits? How much sleep do you get each night? What type of people do you surround yourself with? Do you work in an inviting or toxic workplace? These few questions are just a start in your transformation from sick and tired to healthy and restored, well and rested, and fit and focused. This is where you wanna be! This is where you <u>need</u> to be as a single parent.

*Are you tired of being "sick and tired?" Let me help you get your life in order and get your single parent swag back. Contact me at **april@ singleparentliving.net** to get started!*

It's time to snapback and get your SWAG on!

Single Parent Stigma

Coming From Where I'm From: The stigma of being a single parent follows you around like it's your new BFF. It is inevitable. You can't escape it. Yet, single parenting is what it is. But I be darned if I let it define me and my worth in society and especially in my own home. I am proud to be a single parent because it means I am a survivor and definitely am not a quitter.

My Truth/Turning Point: First and foremost, in order to snapback from society's "single parent stigma" you must truly understand that it is a "you" vs. "them" mentality. You—the single parent vs. them—society at large, the married ones, the system, etc. Get over the fact that you're not invited and/or are not truly welcomed to be in "their" group because you are *a single parent.* Even if *they* do decide to let you in, on those rare occasions, it's only to get a sneak peak because you are "the single one"—and ultimately could pose a threat to their existence (but only to the insecure married ones or those seemingly "in power"). So what is a single parent to do? Should you continue to coward in the shadows or "stand down" while in the presence of couples? Will you be belittled with the stigma associated with the latest statistics and data on single parenting that doom your children to a life of failure and defeat? Do you tolerate the blatant exclusion experienced at the hand of the "fortunate" married ones? NO! You cannot let the stigma define you. Many of today's statistics about single parent homes are depressing and demeaning. Yes, some of the facts are indeed true. But as a single parent in transition for

your snapback, <u>you</u> control the destiny of your children's future—
not a quarterly, government report. With every decision you make
that defies the odds of single parenting, you begin to set a new
single parent standard. When you choose to sacrifice by any means
necessary, you choose to set a new single parent standard. When you
choose to think outside the box and go against the norm, you raise
the bar a little higher. When you choose to keep on doing the right
thing instead of giving up, you become the single parent exception.
Be the exception to the rule. Choose this day to settle or set a higher
standard for single parent living. Single parents and their children
beat the odds every day. Just ask Barack Obama. What greater role
than President of the United States of America, to show that it can
be done?! Look at the success of Gabrielle Douglas. What greater role
than an Olympian representing your country doing the very thing
that you love, to show single parenting success?! The list goes on and
on of single parent households that have proudly produced fierce,
focused and talented children that help make America what it is
today.

Shake off that single parent stigma and be the exception!

Single Parent Survival

Coming From Where I'm From: In order to survive single parenting you must think like a parent but act like a child.

My Truth/Turning Point: Truth is, as I enter into my early 40's, I've found that the key to my single parent survival is simple. Think like a parent, act like a child. Let's examine this a little further shall we? When I fully understood this single parent principle, I became stronger—my will, my mind, my body and my soul. I began to look at life through the eyes of my children. Children in general are happy and carefree. They dream big dreams and think nothing is impossible. Their innocence greets each and every day as if it was the first day of their existence. As a child, their faith in the common good of people is unshakable. Children are open to all possibilities in any given situation. They don't really care or stress out about much. It doesn't matter how they look, the color of their friend's skin, the kind of car they ride in, etc. Now, I'm not saying to live your life in a state of oblivious glee, denying the truth and not facing the facts. But I am encouraging single parents to not take life so seriously. Instead of stressing out, give yourself a "time out" to gather your thoughts and make a plan. When you feel like giving up, go ahead and cry. Have a fit. Throw yourself a "pity-pouty" party every now and then. Yes, it is ok to vent and let off some steam. Scream if you have to. It's okay as long as you don't dwell there too long. So, don't be afraid to take some time to get it together. Time outs and "pity-pouty" parties are not just for kids anymore. Hey, single parents are under a lot of stress. You need to release that stress or you will explode. Trust me, it won't be a pretty picture. You see it all the time where single parents are pushed to their limit and all that is in their path (usually their children) feel the wrath in their hurtful words and your fateful actions. So before you say something you can't take back or before you do something that you may regret for the rest of your life, go into survival mode. Do what kids do—throw a fit, go have a "time out" by yourself, cry until there are no more tears, or shrug your shoulder and don't let the mess of the world get you down. Instead, think happy thoughts like a kid (rainbows, unicorns, ice cream, etc.). I know it may sound simplistic or downright silly, but sometimes single parents do take things too seriously. *Every*thing really isn't that serious. I've learned that an occasional self-imposed "time out" can really help turn things around—for the better. Many times while wallowing in my own pity party, I've emerged with a whole new perspective on life. So, yes, it's ok to act like a kid. I encourage you to fully embrace their carefree mindset and happy-go-lucky mentality (within reason, of course). Kids don't overthink things. Kids just do it without considering the consequences—as long as it makes them happy. And a kid-like happiness is not temporary, but it's a giddy type of happy that has you smiling throughout your day or week. Kids can escape in their minds at a moment's notice. They daydream and wish upon a star at any time of the day or night. You can, too, as a single parent—as long as it isn't *all* day or taking the place of handling real-life responsibilities. I encourage you to embrace your child's way of thinking—keep it simple. A lot of what you worry about isn't worth it anyway. Don't take things personal, keep in mind that whatever you are going through will pass. Most people won't even remember what happened last week or last month. You better believe that the person that hurt you has moved on. So it's time for you to move on, too. You don't see kids stressing out on the playground or threatening to kill someone over something that was said (well, not usually). You've seen it time and time again where girls bicker and boys fight on a Monday, only to end up being BFFs again by Wednesday—like nothing ever happened. Now, I know as adults, it may be harder to "let bygones be bygones." But I'm telling you from experience, the key to single parent survival is to let go, let it go, let . . . it . . . go! Forgive and move forward—just like a child. Keep it simple—just like kids do.

Single Parent Survival Tip: "*Think* like a parent, *Act* like a child!"

Single Parent Swag

Coming From Where I'm From: Who says single parents don't have SWAG? Just because you don't have a rock on your finger doesn't mean you can't put a ring on it—yourself. Now that's SWAG! If you don't have a mate at your side, it doesn't mean you're not complete. It just means you're defining a new standard of SWAG—a Single Parent SWAG! Just because you always have one or more children in tow at all times, doesn't mean you're always on the prowl looking for a mate to help you "make ends meet". The old adage still rings true today "I can do bad all by myself." *Real* single parents honor this truth and in doing so, they honor themselves, too. Now that's SWAG! Why, when you arrive alone at an event, do people automatically assume that you must be lonely and give you the "pity-the-single-parent" look? Honestly speaking, these are the type of single parents who tend to *have* the most SWAG—you don't travel in a pack. You're secure in traveling solo, baby!

My Truth/Turning Point: For some single parents, your journey from snapback to SWAG may be easier than others. Maybe you've always stepped to your own beat. You see things differently. For me, clarity is easy because it has always been about the big picture. I am unique and strangely odd—a chameleon of sorts. I adjust well and adapt easily. Hey, I'm an only child. So, when it comes to defining my SWAG, I can take it there instantly—I can turn it up or tone it down depending on the situation. My SWAG at the moment is defined as: **S**trategic, **W**hole, **A**mbitious, **G**ifted. What does your SWAG look like? Does it accurately reflect your current status or do you need to tweak it a bit? For those of you who think single parents could never have SWAG, well I'm here to tell you that you can! I'm here to show you how. Are you ready to get your SWAG on? It's quite simple. Just take the letters in the word S.W.A.G. and using it as an acronym, pick adjectives that describe your current single parent lifestyle. To help you get started or to update your S.W.A.G.ness, see the guide below.

Here are a few examples to help you define your **S.W.A.G.:**

S— Satisfied, Safe, Sexy, Successful, Spicy, Sensational, Selective, Settled, Stable, Solid, Saucy, Seasoned, Secure, Sensitive, Sentimental, Sincere, Strategic, Smooth, Smart, Spirited, Spontaneous, Striking, Strong, Stylish.

W—Witty, Warrior, Wonderful, Worthy, Warm, Whole, Wise.

A— Amazing, Attractive, Ambitious, Accomplished, Accountable, A-game, Advisor, Aspiring, Attentive, Authentic.

G— Gorgeous, Gifted, Genuine, Graceful, "Got Game", "Go-Getter", Glamorous, Goal-oriented, Great.

List **_your_** SWAG below. Next, begin to *honor* and *walk in* it:

S: _____

W: _____

A: _____

G: _____

It's time to get your SWAG on!

About the author

As a single parent advocate, April Boyd-Noronha has coached, blogged and created single parent training and curriculum since 2008 at Single Parent Living, LLC. She is a single parent strategist and source for guidance, inspiration, motivation and training.

She launched *SingleParentLiving.net* in 2008 in the midst of surviving a divorce and becoming a single parent of three children (two daughters and one son). April's passion is to help other single moms and dads find success and serenity in their single parent lifestyle. She has an MBA from Capella University and a Bachelor's degree in Business Administration from the University of Central Missouri. This is April's second book. Her first book *"Good Bosses Gone Bad: How to Survive the Workplace When Your Boss Sucks"* (2012) advises today's employees on how to successfully navigate toxic workplaces.

Follow April at:

Facebook: facebook.com/singleparentliving

Twitter: #singleparent101

LinkedIn: www.linkedin.com/in/aprilboydnoronha/

Phone: (816) 214-3717

Single Parent Living, LLC

P.O. Box 6405

Lee's Summit, Missouri 64064-6405